More Praise for
Change Your Gambling,

"From recognizing the problem to changing your daily patterns to living a life beyond the dream of hitting it big, this book will transform your thinking about gambling and put you on the path to real change and long-term recovery."—Christopher Kennedy Lawford, author, *Symptoms of Withdrawal* and *Moments of Clarity*

"This is a well-written and easily accessible book that provides the tools for individuals to take control of their gambling problem. In an era where professional addiction treatments are common and yet frequently unsuccessful, it is exciting to see a comprehensive, self-directed approach to addiction recovery."—Jon E. Grant, MD, JD, MPH, professor of psychiatry, University of Minnesota School of Medicine, Minneapolis, Minnesota; coauthor, *Pathological Gambling*

"The self-directed approach to addiction recovery is getting the attention it deserves with this must-read book for people who want to work through a gambling problem on their own. Kudos to Dr. Shaffer and his coauthors for meaningfully advancing the problem gambling treatment field with this book."—Ken C. Winters, professor, Department of Psychiatry, University of Minnesota Medical School

"The topics of gambling and gambling problems often lead to politically and emotionally charged discussions that ignore the needs of the small percentage of people who need help. Dr. Shaffer and his colleagues have removed the value judgments and provided a thoughtful, authoritative manual for those in need."—Frank J. Fahrenkopf, Jr., president and CEO, American Gaming Association

"At the Dunes, our clients have seen profound results from using the exercises in the chapters on anxiety and relapse prevention. Dr. Shaffer and his colleagues have come up with a practical way to combat addiction, one thought at a time. Valuable for clients, clinicians, and anyone with an addiction problem."—Madeleine Narvilas, Esq., LMSW, executive director, The Dunes East Hampton

"The authors have devoted decades of time and energy to the study and treatment of people whose gambling has caused them problems. They have condensed and translated this wealth of experience into a book that is state-of-the-science and accessible to all people who want to change their patterns of gambling, whether on their own or with the aid of a professional or self-help group."—Stephen A. Maisto, PhD, ABPP, editor, *Psychology of Addictive Behaviors*; Department of Psychology, Syracuse University

"Bravo! This groundbreaking self-help resource is a boon to millions of excessive gamblers who would do best as captain of their own ship. It is a prototype that will be replicated many times across the broad spectrum of addictive disorders. *Change Your Gambling, Change Your Life* reads like a good friend offering a helping hand, asking for nothing in return. It whets your appetite, then invites you to enjoy any or all of its sumptuous menu." —Harvey B. Milkman, PhD, professor of psychology; director, Center for Interdisciplinary Studies, Metropolitan State College of Denver

"This book is an excellent resource for individuals who struggle with gambling regardless of the severity of their problem. Written clearly and with compassion, it offers various self-help tools to help people find their own pathway to change, always taking into account each person's unique characteristics and preferences."—Michael Levy, PhD, vice president clinical services, CAB Health and Recovery Services and Health and Education Services, Peabody, Massachusetts

"In the summer of 2011, the American Society of Addiction Medicine introduced a revolutionary new definition of addiction that, for the first time, includes the behavioral addictions. Finally, after more than thirty years of research, pathological gambling has come out of the closet! Dr. Shaffer and his colleagues eloquently discuss 'intemperate gambling as a disorder of excess' and provide an invaluable practical roadmap for clinicians, patients, and their loved ones on the road to recovery from gambling addiction."—Petros Levounis, MD, MA, director, The Addiction Institute of New York; associate clinical professor of psychiatry, Columbia University College of Physicians and Surgeons

"If you are struggling with problem gambling, Dr. Shaffer's approach to coping with addictive disorders is based on sound principles and workable solutions. This book will help you if you follow his course of action."—Kitty S. Harris, PhD, LCDC, LMFT, director, Center for the Study of Addiction and Recovery, Texas Tech University

CHANGE YOUR
GAMBLING,
CHANGE YOUR
LIFE

Harvard Health Publications
HARVARD MEDICAL SCHOOL
Trusted advice for a healthier life

CHANGE YOUR GAMBLING, CHANGE YOUR LIFE

STRATEGIES FOR MANAGING YOUR GAMBLING AND IMPROVING YOUR FINANCES, RELATIONSHIPS, AND HEALTH

HOWARD SHAFFER, PhD

with Ryan Martin, PhD, John Kleschinsky, MPH, and Liz Neporent, MA

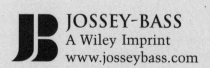

JOSSEY-BASS
A Wiley Imprint
www.josseybass.com

Published by Jossey-Bass
A Wiley Imprint
One Montgomery Street, Suite 1200, San Francisco, CA 94104-4594—www.josseybass.com

Jossey-Bass books and products are available through most bookstores. To contact Jossey-Bass directly call our Customer Care Department within the U.S. at 800-956-7739, outside the U.S. at 317-572-3986, or fax 317-572-4002.

Wiley also publishes its books in a variety of electronic formats and by print-on-demand. Some material included with standard print versions of this book may not be included in e-books or in print-on-demand. If the version of this book that you purchased references media such as CD or DVD that was not included in your purchase, you may download this material at http://booksupport.wiley.com. For more information about Wiley products, visit www.wiley.com.

Library of Congress Cataloging-in-Publication Data
Shaffer, Howard.
    Change your gambling, change your life : strategies for managing your gambling and improving your finances, relationships, and health / Howard Shaffer ; with Ryan Martin, John Kleschinsky, and Liz Neporent. – 1st ed.
        p. cm.
    Includes bibliographical references and index.
    ISBN 978-0-470-93307-7 (pbk.); ISBN 978-1-118-17103-5 (ebk.); ISBN 978-1-118-17104-2 (ebk.); ISBN 978-1-118-17105-9 (ebk.)
    1. Compulsive gambling–Treatment.   2. Compulsive gambling–Psychological aspects.   3. Compulsive gambling–Social aspects.   I. Martin, Ryan.   II. Kleschinsky, John.
III. Neporent, Liz.   IV. Title.
    RC569.5.G35S53 2012
    616.85'84106–dc23

                                                2011042388

Printed in the United States of America
FIRST EDITION
PB Printing   10 9 8 7 6 5 4 3 2 1

To Linda, who continues to teach me to do things on my own;
in addition to her loving support, she sacrificed her time to afford me
the opportunity to work on this project
—HJS

To my parents and my mentors
—RM

To my wife, Melissa, for her limitless love, patience, and support; to my
mother for teaching me the value of service to others; and to those
who seek to change, may you find your path
—JHK

To my wonderful husband, Jay, the love of my life
—LN

Contents

PART THREE How to Stay the Course   187

Preface

We wrote this book as a way to support anyone looking to take a self-help approach to recovery from gambling addiction. We also want to provide support for loved ones and clinicians encouraging such efforts. Our aim is to provide a variety of tried-and-true self-directed tools to help control problem gambling.

Unfortunately, most people with addiction receive a specific kind of help that's primarily determined by the door they knock on to get help rather than by the problem they have. This is particularly common for an expression of addiction like pathological gambling. Even as there are many popular treatments with little or no empirical evidence to support their use, there are many effective and legitimate treatments that are overlooked. Influenced by the assortment of ideas that influence treatment, a help-seeking gambler can sometimes feel like a rudderless ship adrift on an ocean of indifference and misinformation.

We believe that self-directed change is one approach to addiction recovery that is underrated and underutilized. There seems to be a deeply rooted belief in this society, even among some clinicians, that people with addiction can make improvements only with professional help.

In fact, people recover from addiction in many different ways. Some people are comfortable getting help; others prefer to work things out on their own. Across a wide variety of problems, there are more people who want to try to make changes without help compared to those who seek assistance. As the scientific evidence regarding addiction mounts, it's more apparent than ever that behavior change can occur with or without treatment. In fact, the majority of individuals recover via self-directed change.

WHAT IS PATHOLOGICAL GAMBLING?

The American Psychiatric Association (APA) defines pathological gambling as an urge to gamble despite harmful negative consequences or a desire to stop. We prefer to view intemperate gambling as a disorder of excess; that is, as an addiction. The APA's introduction of pathological gambling as a diagnosis in 1980 sparked a new interest in its causes and treatments. Now, more than thirty years later, the study and treatment of gambling problems remains a nascent field with new ideas and approaches emerging all the time.

Although high-quality research is shedding light on gambling and gambling-related conduct all the time, strange beliefs still persist about why someone becomes a problem gambler. For example, some experts, and even some gamblers, tend to think that inanimate objects, such as slot machines, dice, and cards, are the cause of gambling disorders. If these were the necessary and sufficient catalysts for the problem, people wouldn't develop gambling disorders without using them.

However, the opposite is true. The vast majority of people who play slot machines, dice, or cards don't develop a gambling problem, whereas many people who do develop gambling issues never touch any of these objects. For example, some people who struggle to limit their out-of-control bets on sporting events might never succumb to the flashing lights of the slot machines or the lure of a card game.

You might presume that exposure to gambling opportunities is sufficient to jump-start addictive behavior. Research tells us that this isn't always the case either. People tend to adapt relatively quickly after exposure to gambling opportunities, and the prevalence of pathological activity increases only during the short term—as a novelty effect—after the introduction to new gambling opportunities. In other words, there seems to be something about the gambler—as opposed to particular games played or exposure to gambling—that is central to the development of gambling-related problems.

The idea of adaptation to changes in the social setting emerged from the work of Norman Zinberg, a highly influential addiction treatment specialist who recognized the importance of understanding the interactive biological (drug), psychological (set), and social (setting) influences that determine the subjective effects of intoxicant use. Over time, these factors interact to regulate substance use and to limit adverse consequences; simply put, given time, many people with addiction tend to improve even if they do nothing to control their addiction. Zinberg and one of the authors of this book, Howard Shaffer, were the first to generalize these theories about adaptation to gambling, even though most experts were predicting a spike in the rate of pathological gambling as legalized gambling expanded.

In reality, the prevalence of pathological gambling among adults has remained remarkably steady during the past thirty-five years despite an unprecedented increase in access to lotteries, casinos, Internet gambling, and other gambling opportunities. New research even shows a decline in the rate of gambling among young people in recent years. Gambling disorders are far from being relentlessly progressive; rather, research reveals that many individuals move in and out of gambling disorders.

If exposure to gambling opportunities doesn't necessarily contribute to the development of gambling problems, what does? Co-occurring mental health disorders seem to have a significant impact. Research indicates that pathological gamblers are approximately seventeen times more likely than people without gambling problems to have mental disorders, substance use disorders, or both.

SELF-DIRECTED RECOVERY
FROM GAMBLING

People with a gambling disorder are often hesitant to enter treatment, but research shows that they still can manage to improve their situation even without any sort of outside help. The National Epidemiologic Survey on Alcohol and Related Conditions and the National Gambling Impact Study Commission found that, among individuals who previously have experienced pathological gambling during their lifetime, 36 to 39 percent have not experienced any gambling-related problems in the past year, but only 5.5 percent of them received professional treatment for their gambling problems, and only 7.3 percent attended one of the popular self-help group meetings held by Gamblers Anonymous. None of the participants in the National Comorbidity Survey Replication with a pathological gambling diagnosis had received treatment for their problem, even though nearly half had received treatment for other mental disorders.

We recognize that there are many different factors that might make you hesitate to seek help: you may be ashamed of your circumstances; you may be unaware that help is available; you may not have insurance or the financial resources to enter treatment; or you may simply feel that you want to try working things out on your own. Whatever the reason, there should be nothing stopping you from trying to take control and to assume responsibility for your own recovery. We strongly believe that with a few life-threatening exceptions, people deserve the opportunity at least to try to recover on their own if they so choose.

We are not saying that all people with addiction under every circumstance can or should change without having some help. What we do want to emphasize is that the idea that you can't recover and change addiction on your own defies current scientific evidence and magnifies our desire to bring the truth, through first-rate resources and sound advice, to as many people as we can who are suffering with addiction, as well as to their families and the clinicians who try to help them. We believe that simply knowing that you can change on your own permits and even creates new and different opportunities for change.

At the same time, we also want you to know that if you aren't immediately ready to change your addiction, this doesn't mean you won't ever be ready. Similarly, if you do decide you need professional treatment of some kind, or decide you'd do best with a mix of self-help and professionally guided strategies, that's OK too.

Our main premise is that self-directed change is preferable and often successful for many people in recovery from gambling problems. Someone struggling with unrelenting excessive gambling also might be experiencing other mental health problems, such as depression, anxiety, or drug abuse; for this reason, we've devoted a number of chapters to co-occurring problems that are typical for pathological gamblers. Our belief is that success can come from tackling more than one problem at once, or at least having the tools to tackle accompanying issues when you are ready to face them. No one is a helpless victim to excessive gambling.

The bottom line is that there is no "right" way to recover from addiction. We do hope that this book encourages you to accept self-directed change for your gambling problems. We also hope that we've provided more ways to recover than you might have realized were available before you picked up this book.

Acknowledgments

This book was a long time in the making. As a result, a number of people participated in various aspects of manuscript preparation. We acknowledge our colleagues who made central contributions to the development of this book. Sara Kaplan, Ingrid Maurice, Leslie Bosworth, and Erica Marshall were instrumental research assistants who helped organize and prepare early manuscript versions. We appreciate the many gifts they brought to this project and are very proud of their accomplishments since they left the Division on Addiction for greener pastures. We also recognize our colleagues at the Division on Addiction. Tasha Chandler, Debi LaPlante, Sarah Nelson, Richard LaBrie, and Christine Thurmond provided encouragement, support, curiosity, and assistance as we developed this project. For these gifts, we extend our special thanks. We also thank Julie Silver and Linda Konner for their guidance and encouragement as we prepared and revised this book. We thank the late Thomas Cummings for collaborating with Dr. Shaffer for so many years; he enlightened us all about the nature of gambling addiction and how people recover from it. We extend special thanks to Kathy Scanlan and Marlene Warner for their support and collaboration as we worked together to learn from, teach, and treat people struggling with gambling-related problems. Finally, we thank the many gamblers and their families who shared the most intimate details of their lives as they were coping with their gambling-related problems. They taught us well, and for this we are forever grateful.

CHANGE YOUR
GAMBLING,
CHANGE YOUR
LIFE

Introduction: How to Use This Book

There are two major ways to change behavior: change the world around you or change the way you see it. Without our making any assumptions about you, the information in this book is aimed at helping you change both.

The purpose of this book is to help you gain control of your gambling and understand it within the context of the many other issues in your life. Although we want to make sure you understand that changing behavior is difficult, it is not impossible—and you are certainly capable of making tangible, important changes in your life. Yes, gambling may be causing problems for you. You may have tried to get these problems under control many times, or perhaps this is your first time making an attempt. Whatever the circumstances, when you are ready, you will be able to achieve your goals.

Changing your relationship with gambling means sorting out many aspects of your life, gaining some perspective, and acquiring new skills. In many ways, you are taking a journey. This Introduction provides an overview of the book's design and features that will help you on this journey.

As you probably have realized already through your own experience, excessive gambling is born of—and begets—other problems. We have structured this book to help you recognize and cope with your gambling issues as well as your other problems because we believe

1

you'll have the greatest chance of recovery if you make improvements in multiple areas of your life.

THERE ARE NO RULES

Although we've titled this Introduction "How to Use This Book," we have no intention of giving you a list of rules. In fact, you don't have to read the chapters in any special order; you don't even have to read all the chapters. You'll probably determine fairly quickly which information applies to you and which doesn't.

For example, most people with a gambling problem have what psychiatrists call "co-occurring disorders." This is simply a fancy label for the problems you have in your life. Many problem gamblers are plagued with anxiety. Others suffer from depression. Some struggle with substance abuse. Some experience all of these problems. But you may not have any of those challenges; if that's the case, there's no reason to dwell on the chapters that cover those topics, though you might find a quick review of the information in them useful.

You might want to start with a chapter you think is easiest for you to tackle. If you feel confident in your ability to set goals, then the chapter focused on goal setting could be the right place for you to start. Or you might feel the need to tackle a specific problem right away, such as worry about your job or problems at home, or mood swings from day to day. If so, then the chapter focused on solving that particular problem would be a good place for you to start.

The main goal of this book is to guide you toward an approach and solutions to your gambling problems that work for *you*. There is no right way or wrong way to get your gambling under control—only a way that is best for you. You may decide to take a completely self-directed journey; in other words, you can try to conquer your gambling problems and all of the accompanying baggage on your own. However, after you begin reading, you may feel that you need the help of a counselor, therapist, psychologist, or psychiatrist; a self-help or professionally run group; a family member; or a few close friends. Or you may decide on a strategy that combines working on your own with some support from others. Any of these strategies can work in different situations, and this book can be of help.

Although you're certainly capable of facing recovery on your own, there's nothing wrong with reaching out for a helping hand. We certainly encourage you to consider asking for help, especially if you feel overwhelmed with the task of confronting your addiction. Your primary care physician is often a good resource. Similarly, social workers, psychologists, other types of counselors, and various organizations, which we describe in the Resources and Further Reading section, can also provide a wealth of information, help, and resources.

HOW THIS BOOK IS ORGANIZED

The chapters are laid out in three parts: How to Begin, How to Change, and How to Stay the Course.

Part One, How to Begin, is a series of chapters designed to prepare you for what lies ahead. This part of the book will help you evaluate your starting point and how ready you are to make changes.

The chapters in Part Two, How to Change, outline the different approaches to changing behavior. Over the course of more than thirty years of clinical research and patient practice, we have come to the conclusion that there are three main pathways you can consider to overcome a gambling addiction and the problems associated with it:

1. You can do nothing and wait for change to come.
2. You can try to change on your own, using self-help techniques like the ones outlined in this book.
3. You can change with support, including organizations, self-help groups, or a range of supportive and therapeutic professionals.

We refer to each of these choices as a *pathway* because each determines the road you travel to get where you need to go. Because both our research and practice have shown that other problems often accompany gambling and that these difficulties can exacerbate the gambling or get in the way of making change, we go beyond dealing with only the gambling behavior and ask you to work on any issues you might have with anxiety, mood, impulse control, and substance abuse as well.

These chapters also act as toolboxes packed with exercises, strategies, and approaches. Think of the pathways as the roads you travel toward recovery and of the toolboxes as the walking stick, GPS, and other equipment that help you reach your destination successfully. You'll use the tools to stop, delay, or avoid gambling.

These tools fall into three general categories:

1. Managing situations
2. Controlling urges
3. Identifying triggers

Finally, the chapter in Part Three, How to Stay the Course, contains valuable resources for recovery and preventing relapses and slipups. This is a very important part of the book. Even if you complete the chapters appropriate to you and get your gambling under control, at some point in the future you might find yourself at risk for slipping into old ways. That's why we've included information in the Resources and Further Reading section that specifically addressees how to prevent backslides and how to deal with the consequences if one occurs. In addition, we've also gathered a diverse list of resources that will help support your efforts now and going forward.

Because you'll probably do some skipping around, we've structured each chapter as a self-contained entity that's relatively uniform and simple. This should make it easy for you to use this book on your own, with a clinician, or with anyone else who is helping you with your recovery. It's also structured so that you can adapt it to your needs and preferences in the ways that make you most comfortable, work best with your life, and ultimately lead to the best results.

It's quite possible that you've already tried some of the suggestions and strategies discussed in this book. Feel free to skip the ones that haven't worked; however, you might want to consider giving approaches that have failed in the past another try. This time could be the charm. Timing is everything, and sometimes a strategy that hasn't helped you in the past will work under new and different circumstances—or simply because you're in a different frame of mind and are truly ready to make the change.

WHERE TO START

Before undertaking such a major and important project as recovery, it's important for you to understand how you feel and what underlying emotions have the potential to distract you from succeeding. You also need to assess your level of comfort with the decisions you are about to make.

Let's begin by having you figure out how you feel right now by taking the following self-assessment. As we do for all the exercises in this book, we recommend that you keep your answers in a special notebook or journal so that all of your work is in one place for you to review and reflect on. If you're using a support team or group, plan on sharing and discussing your responses with them too.

WHERE DO YOU GO FROM HERE?

Armed with your answers to the self-assessment questions and a sense of your current level of comfort, you can now choose to do one of three things:

- Keep reading this book and continue the process of changing your behavior

- Close this book and keep things just as they are for the time being (but maybe come back to it later)
- Close this book and find other ways to change

If you decide you're not ready for change, perhaps you just need to sort out your thoughts and feelings. Sometimes it's best simply to acknowledge this and take some time to understand your decision. If

---

Self-Assessment

1. On this 10-point scale, where 1 represents the calmest or most relaxed you've ever felt and 10 represents the most nervous or tense you've ever felt, circle the number that represents how you feel right now.

    1   2   3   4   5   6   7   8   9   10

2. Are you being honest with yourself about having a problem with gambling?
3. How have you been feeling during the past month? If these feelings are relatively recent, why do you think you are having them now?
4. What has influenced you to decide to make a change in your life and get your gambling and other issues under control?
5. What happened to make you want to change now?
6. Is this your first effort at gaining control of your gambling?
7. What do you think has held you back from making changes in your life?
8. What influences your current gambling behavior?
9. What do you usually do about these influences?
10. What do you want the end result of using this book to be?

Think about the roles different people will play in your recovery: What role will you take? If you're currently under treatment, what role will your provider play? What role will other people in your life play?

---

you feel too nervous or anxious and think you might need some help to calm your feelings before continuing, please flip to Chapter Five for some practical relaxation techniques. Sometimes all it takes is a step back to gain a clearer sense of what you want to accomplish.

If you've decided you're ready to make some changes in your life and you think this book can help you with the process, continue on to Chapter One. It offers a basic overview of what your underlying issues could be and explores the possible reasons for your troubles with gambling.

Part 1

How to Begin

Assessing Your Problems

1

What you'll learn in this chapter: As you think about changing your life, the information in this chapter can help you start the process with some preliminary information about problems with gambling and the other associated mental health issues we cover in the upcoming chapters. It includes descriptions and some general assessment tools to help you figure out which potential problems you might be experiencing in addition to your difficulties with gambling.

WHAT DOES IT MEAN TO BE ADDICTED TO GAMBLING?

It comes as a surprise to some, but you can be addicted to gambling in the same way that you can be addicted to alcohol or drugs. You can be addicted either to a substance, such as cigarettes or alcohol, or to activities, such as gambling or sex. Although there's no precise definition of addiction or single accepted standard of treatment, there are certain ways of describing the experience to help you gain a better understanding.

Certainly gambling problems aren't anything new; people have been writing about these difficulties as far back as 1812, and, reaching even further back into history, there are cave drawings depicting gambling-like behaviors. However, the concept that gambling is more than just a moral defect is relatively new. Most experts and clinicians now consider gambling addiction a legitimate biological, cognitive, and behavioral issue, and problem gambling can both follow from and lead to mental disorders and other problems.

Gambling problems have many potential causes: genetics, erroneous thought patterns, impulse control disorders, poverty, life experiences—these are just a few. Not every issue will apply to your particular relationship with gambling; different gambling-related symptoms and consequences affect each gambler in different ways. An estimated 2 to 3 percent of the U.S. population has experienced some level of gambling-related problem during their lifetime, according to the ongoing National Comorbidity Survey Replication, among other sources. This means that about 2 million people in the United States have experienced some level of gambling disorder; another 3.5 million experience problems with gambling that don't quite meet the "pathological disorder" threshold.

You might express your addiction in different ways depending on the circumstances. For instance, you might drink alcohol all the time or drink only when you go to the track. You might have some occasional difficulties, or you might gamble in a way that disrupts your life on a frequent basis. Some people need treatment to recover from addiction; others seem to recover on their own with no help from anyone. When mental health experts talk about addiction, they're referring to *addiction syndrome*. This syndrome encompasses a cluster of symptoms and behaviors that stem from the same underlying conditions, but these symptoms are not always present at the same time. The risk factors for developing the addiction syndrome are a complex interaction of genetic, psychological, social, and other factors. For example, someone with a genetic predisposition to addiction who also grows up in an environment that includes available drugs and gambling would be at great risk for developing addiction.

Just like any other expression of addiction, gambling addiction has a recognizable course and typical stages of development that don't necessarily follow the same order or manifest in the same way for everyone. To gain a better understanding of an entire time line of gambling addiction, let's examine one person's journey.

THE STAGES OF ADDICTION

When Courtney was sixteen, an older friend got her a fake ID, and they hit one of the local casinos. There she took her first sip of alcohol. Later that night, her friend urged her to try her hand at blackjack. She picked up the rules of the game easily and did pretty well. The experience made her feel very grown up, and because she didn't get caught or feel sick afterward, she figured it was no big deal. In the language of addiction, this first introduction to the objects of addiction—in Courtney's case, drinking and gambling—is called the *initiation stage*. As Courtney experienced, at this point the risks seemed few and far between and the pleasures obvious, making it all the more likely for her to continue this behavior.

Continue Courtney did. By the time she was of legal age, she was drinking and gambling on a regular basis. Her entire social life revolved around the casinos. She enjoyed both activities immensely, especially when she drank and gambled at the same time. She had entered what is known as the *precontemplation stage*, the point where the person feels pleasure as she continues her use of a substance or becomes more involved in an activity. Although Courtney occasionally gambled a little too much and sometimes ran low on cash, she didn't mind asking her parents or her siblings for a loan to tide her over. She didn't yet view her gambling or drinking as a problem, so why change?

Then one night, she had too much to drink, bet big, and lost more than a month's salary. She woke up the next morning flat broke with a terrible hangover. This time when she asked her parents for money, they were furious. As her mother sobbed, her father lectured her that this would be the last time they would write her a bailout check. When she looked for sympathy from her brother and sister, she realized that they too were fed up. It felt as if her entire family had turned against her; this was both humiliating and terrifying.

As Courtney drove home from her parents', it struck her that she had no money, had alienated her loved ones, and often woke up feeling sick and queasy. This certainly wasn't how she dreamed her life would be. It was in this *contemplation stage* of addiction that Courtney realized she longed to change. She began to imagine what it would be like if she were to quit drinking and stay away from the blackjack tables. After several months of thinking about it—during which time she continued to feel even worse and lose even more money—she finally entered the *preparation stage*, when she began to attempt to get her life back under control.

Courtney eventually entered the *active quitting stage*: she began to put a lot of energy into quitting drinking and gambling. Besides going to group meetings, she set some concrete goals for herself, stuck to a strict schedule, and took up yoga to help her relax and get in shape. Any time she felt the urge to take a drink or take a run through the tables, she'd call a nongambling friend and invite her to a meal or a yoga class to help keep distracted. Sometimes her preventive strategies worked. Occasionally she slipped up. But she was determined to make improvements and, after nearly two years of hard work, she found herself in the *maintenance stage*, also known as *relapse prevention*. Finally her life seemed under control. She was out of debt. She felt and looked better. Her parents and siblings were proud of her progress, and her relationships with them had greatly improved. She honestly didn't know that she'd never again take another drink or lay down another card, but she felt sure of her priorities now and knew she was better off for the changes she'd made.

Not everyone goes through every stage of addiction and recovery in exactly the same way as Courtney did. Some people never see their addiction as an issue. Some never try to change even after they begin to have problems. It's also not uncommon for someone to try to quit his addiction several times before he's successful.

ARE YOU STRUGGLING WITH GAMBLING ADDICTION?

As you begin to think about the process of change, you may find it helpful to get a feel for your own relationship with gambling. To do this, take out your journal and write down your thoughts about the following questions:

- Do you become restless, irritable, or anxious when trying to stop or cut down on gambling?
- Have you tried to keep your gambling a secret from your loved ones?
- Has your gambling resulted in financial problems?

If your answer is yes to any one of these questions, it's likely that you have problems with gambling. Even if you answered no to all three questions, if you feel concerned about the consequences of your gambling and how it affects your life, you have a gambling problem.

Experts often rate health problems on a scale. For example, we use a 0–3 scale to assign levels to a gambling problem. Someone who is currently abstaining from gambling completely is labeled a 0. Someone who is gambling but isn't experiencing any negative consequences because of it is labeled a 1. Someone who is gambling and experiencing some negative consequences but not enough to consider that she has a gambling disorder per se is labeled a 2. And someone who is experiencing sufficiently negative consequences to merit serious changes and possible treatment is labeled a 3.

Gamblers often transition back and forth between healthy and unhealthy levels of gambling. The length of time that someone stays at a specific gambling level varies, and level 2 is the stage where things usually either get better or worse; however, some people languish at level 2 and suffer with some gambling problems for an extended period of time.

Think about this scale for a moment. Ask yourself how you would label your difficulties with gambling at various points in your life. Where are you right now on this scale? Maybe you've tried to get your gambling under control before, transitioned up a level, but then reverted back to your current level. Write down your answers to these questions in your journal.

If you are at a level that describes your behavior as problematic, take heart. This book, as well as other recovery and change strategies, can help you gain control. If gambling or the consequences of your gambling are causing you to worry, think of this as an opportunity. Worry can be an engine that drives change.

WHAT OTHER PROBLEMS ARE YOU EXPERIENCING?

As we mentioned earlier, gambling can be a part of an addiction syndrome or be accompanied by a host of other mental health issues. You may have some symptoms that are associated with a particular problem, but perhaps these symptoms don't reflect a full-blown disorder. It's possible to experience some symptoms without suffering from the full expression of the illness. In fact, most people have some symptoms that are commonly associated with an emotional disorder at some point in their lives even if they can't be clearly diagnosed.

To help you clarify what your issues might be, we've included some brief descriptions of problems and associated symptoms that commonly overlap with gambling addiction. All of them are described in greater detail in upcoming chapters along with some suggested strategies for helping you get them under control. It's likely that you are experiencing one or two or even several of these issues, but don't let that scare you. Knowing what you may be struggling with is a good thing: it allows you to understand your problems and your specific needs, and that brings you one step closer to finding a solution. When reading these descriptions, keep in mind that only a trained clinician can make a clinical diagnosis.

Anxiety Disorders

Anxiety is a sense of worry that doesn't seem rational. When you are anxious, you feel concern that you'll somehow lose control or that bad things are coming your way, but you don't quite know why you feel like this. Because anxiety can be very uncomfortable, some people get involved with activities that distract them from these feelings. Gamblers often gamble when they feel the need to defuse a high level of anxiety. When you're anxious a lot, doctors say that you have an anxiety disorder. There are many manifestations of an anxiety disorder, some of which are described in the next sections. If you're concerned that you might have some issues with anxiety and that perhaps they are contributing to your problems with gambling, you may find the information in Chapter Five helpful. It provides a more in-depth look at anxiety as well as opportunities to learn more about getting anxiety under control.

Obsessive-Compulsive Disorder

People with obsessive-compulsive disorder (OCD) have repeated, frequent obsessions and compulsions that interfere with their ability to function normally. Obsessions are repeated and unwanted thoughts and impulses that cause distress or anxiety. For example, a person might be hyperfocused on germs for fear they might cause disease, or on the tangled fringe on the rug because it spoils the organization of the room. Compulsions are repeated behaviors or rituals that are difficult to stop. To control germs, an obsessive-compulsive person might wash his hands repeatedly; to deal with the rug fringe, he might continually straighten it. Sometimes people gamble because they are obsessive-compulsive. For someone like this, gambling is very difficult to stop.

Post-Traumatic Stress Disorder

Although this is a mental disorder that's often associated with soldiers, post-traumatic stress disorder (PTSD) can result from any traumatic event, situation, or experience. People who experience PTSD have frequent thoughts and feelings about the event and may have trouble sleeping; when they do sleep, they may dream about it too. People with PTSD tend to startle easily and feel a high degree of distress when anything reminds them of the event. Gambling can become an effective distraction that offers temporary relief from the discomforts associated with PTSD.

Generalized Anxiety Disorder

Generalized anxiety disorder (GAD) is characterized by constant and excessive worries that continue for a long period of time (six months or more) and are difficult to stop. With this worry comes a feeling of edginess, difficulty focusing, irritability, muscle tension, and insomnia. People with GAD might experience a pounding heart, sweating, and trembling.

Social Anxiety Disorder

This is similar to GAD except that it is specifically centered on social situations. Often people with this issue simply avoid social settings even if there's a low risk of embarrassment.

Panic Disorder

Panic attacks are the major symptom of a panic disorder. Panic attacks are characterized by intense fear of, for example, dying or losing control. This discomfort lasts for about twenty minutes or so and, during that time, a person experiencing the panic attack often feels her heart pound, and she sweats profusely; she also may tremble and feel short of breath.

Specific Phobia

A phobia is a persistent fear of specific objects or situations. More than five hundred phobias have been identified; it's possible to be phobic about almost anything, from spiders to heights to elevators. Any exposure to an object or situation that triggers a phobic reaction can cause anxiety. If a phobia is intense enough, it can be highly intrusive and interfere with your life.

Mood Disorders

Everyone experiences changing moods, but when moods become increasingly difficult to handle or you feel that moodiness and emotions contribute to why and when you gamble, it's possible that you have a mood disorder. A mood disorder is a sustained, prolonged mood disturbance, such that your moods and emotions begin to intrude on and restrict your life. If you feel that you are struggling with moods or that your moods contribute to your gambling, you'll find Chapter Six very helpful. It covers the mood disorders we discuss here and provides strategies for helping get them under control.

Major Depressive Disorder (Depression)

Major depressive disorder (MDD) is characterized by at least one clinically significant depressive episode but no manic (intensely active) episodes. Individuals with MDD sometimes struggle with fatigue, poor concentration, lack of sleep, little interest in life activities, and suicidal thoughts. MDD symptoms often are long lasting and interfere with the ability to live a normal life. Those with the milder form of this problem, dysthymic disorder, experience similar symptoms and feelings, but they aren't as intense or long lasting. The stimulating effects of gambling can temporarily reduce the melancholy associated with depression.

Bipolar Disorder

Those with bipolar disorder struggle with extreme mood swings; they either feel extremely depressed or extremely energetic and active (manic). These swings often make it challenging to have normal emotional reactions to average, everyday situations. During depressive periods, people with bipolar disorder may feel suicidal, hopeless, and unable to enjoy life; they'll often complain of insomnia and fatigue. During the manic phase, an inflated sense of self-esteem can lead them to risky and disruptive behavior, such as excessive drinking, drug use, and yes, out-of-control gambling. Increased energy makes it difficult to sleep or focus on responsibilities.

Cyclothymic disorder is a milder form of bipolar disorder. This disorder is characterized by symptoms similar to bipolar disorder, though these symptoms are less severe and do not last as long.

Impulse Control

People with impulse control disorders (ICDs) are unable to control their urges to do certain things, and doing these things helps them release tension and feel a sense of pleasure and gratification. Some common ICDs include trichotillomania, excessive pulling out of hair; pyromania, purposefully starting multiple fires on various occasions; kleptomania, repeatedly stealing objects that are not really needed; and intermittent explosive disorder, being unable to resist the urge to be aggressive.

Problems with excessive gambling certainly can fall into the category of problems with impulse control, and they are often accompanied by other impulse control problems. Whether your gambling addiction is related to a multitude of other issues or to gambling alone, you'll benefit from reading Chapter Seven. It gives in-depth descriptions of impulse control difficulties as well as suggestions for getting them under control.

Substance Abuse

Diagnostically, clinicians classify people as either substance dependent or as having substance abuse issues when they have trouble regulating their use of one or more psychoactive substances, such as alcohol or other drugs (whether legal, prescription, or illegal). People with substance use disorders take more of the substance than recommended. They try to quit but can't, and often spend a lot of time trying to get the substance and recovering from its effects. Their drug use disrupts other important aspects of their life, and often they continue taking the substance even after it obviously begins to create problems in their life.

There are two important and related considerations with substance dependence: tolerance and withdrawal. Those who have tolerance increase their drug use so that they can feel the way they used to on a lower dose. For example, someone using heroin might need increasingly larger dosages to get high because he gradually becomes tolerant to its effects. Withdrawal occurs among people who have ramped up their tolerance and then reduce or stop taking their drug. Once they stop using, the withdrawal symptoms are specific and stereotypical for the particular drug they have been using. For example, a long-term excessive drinker who tries to quit might experience anxiety, tremors, stomach distress, and delirium. In some cases, withdrawal symptoms are so severe that they can become life threatening.

Many gamblers also struggle with substance abuse. If you think you have such issues, we encourage you to read Chapter Eight, which outlines the various strategies for dealing with substance abuse.

WHERE DO YOU GO FROM HERE?

Now that you have a basic idea of how gambling and other possible issues might be disrupting your life, you must decide what you want to do about it. You can certainly close this book and do nothing further. You can continue reading and learn about the self-help approaches to recovery in the upcoming chapters. You can seek guidance from a mental health professional and perhaps attend some group meetings as well. Or you can resolve to try a combination of change strategies.

Whatever you choose to do, by reading this chapter and learning more about the problems in your life, you've already moved closer to recovery. This is an excellent first step. We certainly hope you take the next one—and the next. Just knowing recovery is possible and that you have the ability to make it happen can be a very powerful motivator indeed.

2

Connecting the Dots

What you'll learn in this chapter: Assumptions can be a help or a hindrance. Approaching a problem—be it gambling or anything else—from a different angle can sometimes be the key to its solution. If you think about it, most of what you consider as knowledge is really conventional wisdom or ingrained assumptions. It's these assumptions, these perceptions of the world, that shape your actions and reactions. We'd like to help you rethink your assumptions and perhaps even turn some of them on their ear. Once you can do that, you begin to open yourself up to the possibility of trying new things—or even approaching old things in new ways. Let's start with a brainteaser.

THE NINE DOT PROBLEM

The following diagram is often referred to as the Nine Dot Problem. Study it and then try to connect all nine dots using only four straight lines and without lifting your pen off the paper. Do not look ahead at the solution and attempted solutions.

The Nine Dot Problem

The next figures illustrate four typical attempts to solve the problem.

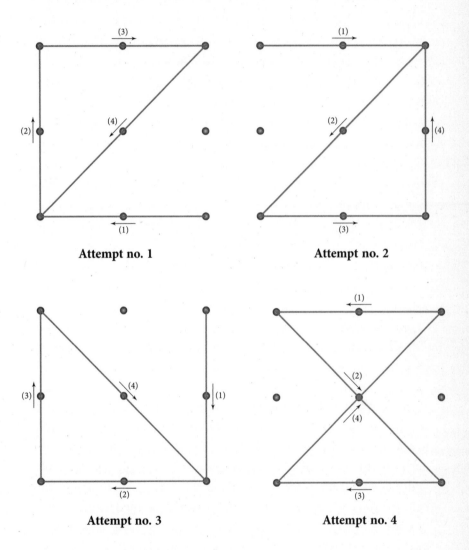

Attempt no. 1

Attempt no. 2

Attempt no. 3

Attempt no. 4

All of these are typical guesses, but none are correct. The first three leave out a single dot, and the fourth example leaves out two dots. Keep trying. Give yourself another few minutes, and if you still haven't figured it out, flip the page for the correct solution.

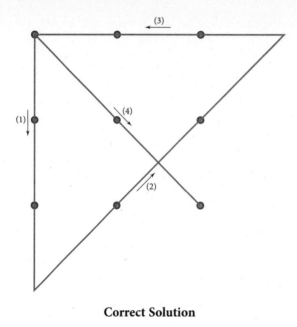

Correct Solution

So let's think about this for a moment. How did you approach solving the problem? What assumptions did you make as you started to search for a solution? For example, your first assumption may have been that the problem was indeed solvable; yes, it might be difficult and you might hit a few snags along the way, but ultimately you believed you could prevail. Or you might have assumed that the solution was simple, but when you couldn't come up with the answer right away, you realized that the problem was more challenging than you originally thought. Or maybe you viewed each new starting point as a new strategy when this was not necessarily the case.

The takeaway here is that some of your assumptions are probably helpful and some probably aren't. This is true whether you are trying to solve a brainteaser or some of life's important problems. For example, the majority of people—96 percent—who have had lifelong problems with gambling also have at least one other psychological issue. It's important to realize that there are different ways of thinking about this relationship—just as there are different ways of thinking about how to connect a series of dots. Your gambling-related behavior can put you at risk for developing other emotional issues, your emotional state can put you at risk for having problems with gambling, or one thing may have nothing to do with the other.

This book can help you put aside your ingrained thinking and get a handle on what is going on in your life. Once you do that, you are on your way to productive solutions to your problems.

WHAT YOU CAN LEARN FROM THE NINE DOT PROBLEM

Were you annoyed by the Nine Dot Problem? Were you irritated that a puzzle that appeared so simple at first was actually quite difficult to solve? If so, that tells you something important about yourself: if you're aggravated by a task that involves connecting the dots, imagine how frustrated and discouraged you might get when trying to deal with personal problems that are as complex as excessive gambling or the other emotional difficulties you're going through.

The Nine Dot Problem gave you a glimpse into how you approach challenges in your life and how your assumptions and approaches can either help or hurt you. When you're trying to conquer a problem and hit a roadblock, it's often tough to stay positive and imagine that things will get better. And it's often scary to take the leap of faith necessary to make real, positive changes.

It's important to know yourself, but at the same time it's important to believe that you can make positive changes even if the journey will be long and hard. The path to a better quality of life has many peaks and valleys. There will be good days and bad. Although certain aspects of this process may be a breeze for you, it's important to understand that getting gambling problems under control will take serious time and effort.

If you experience doubt, fear, anger, resentment, or any other profound emotions as you think about facing your gambling and your other problems, know that these feelings are completely normal. Realize that you've already taken the first significant step toward a better life by picking up this book. If you stay focused and use the techniques we've outlined in the upcoming chapters (and perhaps draw from other sources of support), you will find that *your problems are solvable.*

WHERE DO YOU GO FROM HERE?

One of the key virtues of this book is its emphasis on the importance of looking at your problems as an integrated whole. We believe that it's impossible to separate behaviors or emotions by their sources because, in the end, they are all interconnected. Instead of trying to tease them apart and fix them individually, think of yourself as a person—not as a collection of disorders.

This book can be an excellent way to help manage your gambling behaviors and associated problems, but it's only one of many possible ways to get your life under control. If you decide you're interested in seeking support for your problems, the Resources and Further Reading section provides information about professionals, organizations, and other resources that can also be of help.

We included the Nine Dot Problem and the subsequent examination of your possible assumptions to help you recognize the many ways your thoughts can influence your behaviors. As you go through the rest of the exercises in this book, keep in mind how assumptions can either move you forward or hold you back as you attempt to make significant changes in your life.

3 Setting Goals to Help You Change

What you'll learn in this chapter: Before you review the information in the upcoming chapters, we'd like you to step back for a moment and examine your priorities. If you've never done this before, this exercise will help crystallize your reasons for wanting to change your life. Even if you have some experience with setting goals, this is an exercise worth doing because it can help remind you of what's important and what you're working toward.

Close your eyes, take a deep breath, and think about a day that is trouble free—no gambling problems and no other significant problems. Envision where you would spend this day, what you would do and with whom. Think about how wonderful it would be to have a day like this. Now open your eyes and ask yourself this question: *What's keeping me from having a pleasant day?*

Even if you can't quite picture this lovely day, perhaps you can think back to a time before gambling had an impact on your life. It's likely that you spent your time differently and in different places. The people who influenced you then are not the same people who influence you now. In your current situation, you might not be focused on the same set of priorities.

You don't have to be ill to give self-help techniques a try. Even healthy people benefit from directing their own change. For anything you'd like to change about yourself, self-help is always an option.

A priority is anything that has personal significance. Some common priorities include family, relationships, health, education, and making a difference in the world. Gambling, as well as the other issues that brought you to this book, might be a current priority that is interfering with more important life priorities.

If you haven't given your priorities much thought lately, take out your journal and spend a few moments now listing them. Really think about what they are. This is an extremely important exercise in terms of setting your goals for recovery because priorities help keep you motivated, especially when the going gets tough and you begin to wonder if the hardships you endure to change your life are worth it. Once you gain control of your gambling and other issues in your life, you will be able to put your most important priorities front and center.

WHAT YOU NEED TO KNOW ABOUT GOAL SETTING

Learning to set realistic goals and then work toward these targets is an important skill. Goals play a key role in changing your life because they help you clarify what you want to change—that is, your priorities. It's easier to plan and take steps in the right direction when you know what you're working toward. This is why we ask you to think about your goals before you dive into the details of your specific problems, as you will in the chapters that follow. Can you move toward recovery without goals? Yes. But most people find it much easier to move forward when they are moving toward something instead of away from something.

You may have set goals at some point or another during your life simply by tossing out an idea or going so far as to jot down a few words or intentions on a piece of paper. We are going to take this idea quite a bit further than you may have in the past, by walking you through a series of detailed steps that will force you to get laser focused about what you are trying to accomplish. Once again, we ask you to get out your journal and do some work. Here are some helpful guidelines to keep in mind; these suggestions will increase the chances of coming up with objectives that are both meaningful and attainable.

You might be interested in the cause of your issues. However, you don't always need to determine the cause of problems to reduce the difficulties that these problems create. This book does not ask you to think about ultimate causes, only about how your life is now and how you'd like it to change in the future.

Set Your Large Goals First

Ask yourself what you ultimately want to accomplish. Think about what is most important to you and what will create useful changes in your life. You might have only one main goal in mind, such as controlling your gambling. Or you might have some additional goals, such as to get your anxiety and substance use under control too. Give this a good deal of thought. Make your goals meaningful and manageable.

Take One Step at a Time

Think about a stack of logs blocking a stream. You can't move all the logs at once. But if you wiggle one log loose and it's the right log, you can get them all flowing freely downstream. Well, especially important and sizeable goals are a lot like logjams. If you take the approach that you'll tackle your issues one log at a time rather than all at once, they'll seem more manageable. For this reason, we recommend breaking larger goals up into smaller "stepping-stone" goals. An example: if your large goal is to give up gambling entirely— and it is too daunting to take this on in one step—consider making smaller stepping-stone goals by limiting a certain type of gambling or setting a time or spending limit on the amount of gambling you do.

Divide Your Smaller Objectives into Specific Tasks

Once you set realistic goals and break them down into smaller step-ping-stone goals, consider creating a list of specific tasks needed to reach each stepping-stone. If you decided to clean the kitchen, for example, what would it entail? What needs to be cleaned? Do you have the right tools and products to clean properly? How much time do you have to get the job done? Yes, cleaning your kitchen is a mundane task, but the comparison to controlling your gambling is valid. Do you have the skills to manage your triggers? Do you know how to deal with your gambling buddies? What will you do about urges? What can you do to clean up your gambling debts?

Reward Yourself

The success you experience after finishing each task can motivate you to keep striving for even more success. Reward yourself after complet-ing a task by indulging in a special treat, a relaxation break, or a simple moment to reflect on your achievement. By acknowledging your accomplishment, you help strengthen the connection between change and the pleasure of the journey. However, be mindful of the type of reward you choose. Buying a lottery ticket is not the most sensible reward for skipping a trip to the track.

Define Your Wiggle Room

Although you should try to remain as close to your game plan as possible, it's essential to recognize that sometimes situations come up that are beyond your control. Make allowances for the unexpected by leaving some "wiggle room" in the form of extra time, extra steps, or extra work. For example, if you are planning to clean the kitchen, it's a good idea to build in a little extra time in case you find out that the fridge is dirtier than expected. Likewise with gambling: giving up weekend casino trips may be a little more challenging than you anticipated.

If You Need Help, Ask for It

Even though asking for help might seem like a sign of weakness, doing so actually can make you stronger. Sometimes sharing the burden with someone, whether a loved one or a professional, can relieve the burden of unnecessary stress and allow you to forge ahead toward your goals. Reaching out for help could be a necessary stepping-stone to a goal you haven't been able to achieve on your own.

Reevaluate Periodically

From time to time, review your goals. Doing so allows you to assess your successes and failures and, in turn, fine-tune future goals. For example, it can be useful to understand how you accomplished one of your stepping-stone goals: Did you follow your plan precisely? Did you get help along the way? If you didn't meet your objectives, why not? What went wrong? The answers to these questions will enlighten you.

GOAL SETTING, STEP-BY-STEP

Terry is about to embark on her journey toward changing her relationship to gambling. She believes that setting goals will increase her chances of success. She understands that setting meaningful goals takes quite a lot of thought and work; she thinks it will be worth the effort. She has struggled with gambling and depression for more than two decades, so she figures it's worth taking some time to shine a light on what she's trying to achieve.

> No matter how odd or severe your problems seem, there's a good chance there are others out there going through the same thing. Millions of people have different combinations of issues with a variety of symptoms. No matter how different you feel, you're not alone.

Because Terry feels that she isn't able to concentrate on more than one problem at a time, she decides to zero in on her gambling first and leave aside her struggles with mood for now. She can always come back to them later and go through the same goal-setting process for depression. This is a perfectly legitimate strategy for someone who feels too overwhelmed to deal with everything all at once. You can do this too if you feel that you have too many problems to deal with simultaneously. However, don't be afraid to take on more than one problem at the same time if these difficulties are related.

Primary Goals

Terry starts off the goal-setting process by considering what her *primary goals* are for getting her gambling under control; these are her top three objectives. Terry needs to figure out what she ultimately means by recovery and what she hopes to achieve through change. After some consideration, she writes in her journal:

My Primary Goals

1. Abstain entirely from online poker games.

2. Clean up financial debt.

3. Repair and improve relationships with mom and sister.

She also gives a lot of thought about the resources and relationships she has at her disposal that might help her reach each of her objectives. For example, her friend Dave has offered to block the most frequently visited poker sites on her computer to help reduce her temptation to gamble online. She can spend more time with a group of friends who are supportive about her wish to stop gambling; one of those friends is a financial planner who has promised to sit down with Terry and work out a reasonable budget to put her finances back in the black within six months, provided her gambling stays under control. As for family dynamics, she's still pretty close with her brother, Colin, and he's expressed a desire to help her heal the rift with her mother and sister.

Terry is actually quite lucky: she's sure about what she wants out of recovery, and both her support system and her resources seem extensive. Now what about you? Think through what your primary goals are for getting your gambling under control and write them down in your journal. Then list all of the resources and relationships you think might be helpful in the process. You will probably find that you have more resources than you realize.

Stepping-Stone Goals

The next step for Terry is to break down her primary goals into a series of smaller stepping-stone goals. Think of a series of small, flat rocks that form a path from one side of a stream to the other so that you don't have to leap across all at once. That's the essence of stepping-stone goals. They're a series of small, manageable objectives that move you closer and closer to your primary goal. That way you don't have to try to get there in one big leap.

Along with each stepping-stone goal, Terry lists the tasks associated with accomplishing each of them. She tries to limit this to no more than three tasks per goal to avoid feeling as though she is biting off more than she can chew. If she finds that a stepping-stone goal requires more than three tasks, she will look to split up the goal so that it's more manageable.

She also selects a small reward to give herself after she completes each of these mini goals. Terry understands how important it is to congratulate herself for a job well done. A sample of her work looks like this:

Primary Goal: Clean up financial debt

Stepping-Stone Goal 1: Abstain from online poker games at home

    Task 1: Keep a one-week diary of online activity to determine pattern of usage and times of day I'm most vulnerable to temptation.

    Task 2: Schedule Dave to come over and block access to games on the computer.

    Task 3: Schedule replacement activities for first 2 weeks (dates with friends during times of day that I am most likely to gamble).

    Reward: Once I finish these tasks I will take the night off, relax, and watch TV.

Terry continues creating her plan in this manner, laying out every stepping-stone goal she thinks she will need to meet to get her closer to her primary goal of cleaning up her debt. When she's done plotting out this goal, she moves on and does the same planning for her other two goals.

Now it's your turn. Take your three primary goals and lay out in your journal the stepping-stone goals the way Terry has. You'll probably have about ten stepping-stone goals per primary goal, but it's fine to have more or fewer than that.

Overcoming Obstacles

Even if you lay out detailed blueprints to meet your primary goals as we're suggesting, you won't be able to anticipate every stumbling block that will pop up along the way. Terry, for instance, didn't expect to have so much trouble figuring out her current budget. She doesn't really have a head for numbers, so she quickly became frustrated with the spreadsheet program she was using to complete this task. She could allow this to derail her—or she could find another way to get the job done. Rather than panic, she got out her journal and broke down this latest stumbling block into a series of manageable steps, just as she did with each of her stepping-stone goals.

Should any unforeseen circumstances arise, having detailed plans mapped out in advance can prevent you from getting derailed. Should you come up against any obstacles, rather than stressing out or giving up, get out your journal and break down the stumbling block into smaller parts; then create specific tasks for pushing past the obstacle. More often than not, you will find that what's standing in your way is easier to work around than it first appeared. Once past it, you can keep moving toward change and, ultimately, recovery. And don't forget to reward yourself with something unrelated to gambling once you solve a problem—you deserve it!

Stumbling Block: Can't understand how to create a budget

Task 1: Borrow spreadsheet book from Debbie.

Task 2: Read through book and try some practice sheets.

Task 3: Schedule tutoring session with Debbie.

Reward: Once I finish these tasks, I will treat Debbie to a home-cooked dinner!

SUMMING UP GOAL SETTING

It takes practice and work to achieve your aims, but creating specific, measurable, and achievable tasks and goals is a powerful motivator. Achieving your goals is rewarding, and rewards shape behavior. *You* decide what you want, how to get there, and how much progress you want to make.

If you find that you are failing to reach certain goals, go back to reexamine them. Make sure that you state your goals realistically; readjust your plan if necessary. If need be, break your main goals down into even smaller stepping-stone goals, and your stepping-stone goals into even smaller, more manageable tasks. Determining what hasn't worked so far will help guide you in the future. Getting just a taste of success, even if it's an easy accomplishment, can give you the motivation to continue.

Don't skip the task rewards. Far from trivial, they're an important aspect of the goal-setting process, one that people often overlook or minimize. Rewarding yourself helps create a positive association between the process of working toward your goals and actually meeting them. Just be careful that the rewards aren't out of scale with the accomplishment and that you don't reward yourself with something related to gambling. Also, it's counterproductive to withhold something or punish yourself if you don't meet a goal. Setbacks shouldn't be connected with punishment or negative consequences because this can put you off from trying again. You'll stay inspired if you remain as consistently positive as possible. If you fail, start again. Go back through the goal-setting process and refine it so that you have a better chance of getting to where you want to go.

WHERE DO YOU GO FROM HERE?

We hope that this chapter sparks your motivation to make some positive changes in your life. After reading about the necessary goal-setting skills to help get your gambling and the rest of your life under control, you should now have some direction. With the help of this book and your other resources, you *can* reach your goals—just look at Terry's latest journal entry.

My Accomplishments
Primary Goal: Abstain from online gaming
Date Achieved: June 1st
Achieving this goal made me feel: A mixture of relief, pride, happiness, and accomplishment! I see now that if I take a systematic approach toward my life, my recovery, and my goals, I can achieve anything!
Reward: Begin contribution to company retirement plan.

Part 2

How to Change

4

Getting Your Gambling Under Control

What you'll learn in this chapter: This chapter is concerned with identifying the different levels of gambling and focuses on self-help techniques for change, giving you specific ways to deal with the problems related to gambling. We also help you consider the pros and cons related to seeking professional care.

Gambling is any type of activity that involves risking something of value on an uncertain outcome—an outcome determined by chance. You can gamble on games of chance, such as the lottery, bingo, or dice; or on games of skill, such as sporting events, or even games of skill you play yourself (such as golf or billiards). With games of chance, the odds of winning a particular game are always the same and never change no matter how many times you play; you have no control over the outcome of events, and you can't do anything to increase your odds of winning. You might believe that performing such actions as holding a lucky coin, sitting at a particular table, or blowing on the dice help influence the outcome; this is just superstitious behavior, an illusion of control. With games of skill, your knowledge and experience can influence your odds of winning to some extent, though they certainly can't ever guarantee it.

For most people, gambling is nothing more than a bit of escapist entertainment. However, for a small percentage of the population, gambling becomes difficult to control and can lead to negative consequences; for some, their gambling is so out of control that it has effectively ruined their lives and the lives of many people around them. Although no one knows exactly why some people have more trouble than others stopping excessive and repetitive behaviors like gambling, research has found that genetic predispositions and chemical changes in the brain play a significant role; social events, personality, and emotional disorders also play important roles.

Review the Four Levels of Gambling box to determine which category of gambling you fall into. As noted in Chapter One, it's possible that you have other problems that go hand in hand with gambling. For example, excessive gamblers often struggle with issues that are caused by, influenced by, or in some way related to how much they gamble. Many problem gamblers struggle with anxiety, mood disorders, impulse control disorders, and substance abuse. This is why we cover these issues in great detail in subsequent chapters; sometimes it isn't enough to address gambling problems alone.

THE FOUR LEVELS OF GAMBLING

Level 0: People who don't gamble.

Level 1: People who gamble and experience no negative consequences.

Level 2: People who struggle with gambling and have some problems in their life because they gamble, even though they might not meet the clinical criteria for the most serious form of gambling disorder. Level 2 gamblers frequently are moving in one of two directions: either toward a worsening gambling problem or toward more control of their gambling.

Level 3: People who gamble with enough lack of control and negative consequences to meet the diagnostic criteria for problem gambling.

WHAT IS PROBLEM GAMBLING?

Gary is hooked on gambling. He regularly plays the lottery, bets on all kinds of sports events, and joins just about any card game he can find. When he's not gambling, he's thinking about his next set of bets or plotting a way to get more gambling money. Lately he's stepped up the pace and stakes of his gambling, placing bigger and more frequent bets. That seems to be the only way to feel the rush of excitement he used to feel all the time when he first started gambling as a teen.

Gambling has definitely had an impact on Gary's finances. Even though he couldn't make rent a few months ago, he bet what cash he had on a big football playoff game—and lost. He was forced to borrow money from his brother, who would give him a loan only on the condition that he curtail his gambling. Naturally he agreed to this stipulation. He truly intended to honor it.

> The truth all gamblers need to face is that it's impossible to predict with certainty when the next win will occur. Just because you've been gambling for hours and have not won anything does not mean the next ticket, pull, race, game, or hand will be a winner. The odds of winning remain exactly the same no matter how many times you gamble.

Still, a few days after trying to go cold turkey, he began to feel restless and irritable. When one of his gambling friends told him about a "sure thing" bet on a college basketball game, he couldn't resist. He bet big. He lost big.

Now he's frantically chasing his losses, desperate to win back the rent money his brother loaned him plus enough to keep him going until his next paycheck. He's afraid that if his brother finds out how deep his problems with gambling actually are, he'll cut him off financially and emotionally; Gary's already begun spinning a story about how his apartment was broken into, hoping this will be believable enough to cover his tracks and allow him to ask for more money.

Why Gary started gambling in the first place is difficult to say. He's always had trouble controlling his impulses and has gone through periods of heavy drinking. Gambling seems to ease his anxiety, at least temporarily; and, ironically, it helps him forget about his mounting debt and strained relationships, even if for just a few hours at a stretch. He understands that gambling is a damaging force in his life, yet he can't seem to stop.

Gary is now at a crossroads. If he continues to gamble, especially at this escalating pace, he could lose his family, his job, and his home. He's already in dire straits financially. Gambling more will dig him a deeper hole. Yet the thought of giving up gambling or even slowing down his pace terrifies him. Even if he were able to manage his gambling—which he's not confident he will be able to do—that would mean facing all the other problems in his life. He's also afraid of breaking away from his network of gambling friends. Currently they're his largest social circle; he's concerned he'll feel lonely and isolated without them.

Does Gary's situation sound familiar? If you find yourself preoccupied with gambling, unable to control how much you gamble, or continuing to gamble even after you mount up considerable losses, these are signs that you could have a gambling disorder. Other signs include feeling anxious and irritable when you try to reduce the amount you gamble, lying about your gambling, and experiencing negative financial and personal consequences as a result of gambling. Some people with a gambling disorder find themselves in legal trouble; out of desperation they sometimes lie, steal, or commit crimes (fraud or forgery) to get more gambling money.

MODERATION VERSUS ABSTINENCE

There are two primary strategies for controlling your gambling: you can cut back on your activities, or you can stop entirely. As Gary thinks about what gambling has done to his life, he considers the pros and cons of both approaches.

Limiting the amount and frequency of bets or confining himself to one type of gambling might leave Gary with enough money to get out of debt; it might mean he's better able to concentrate at his job and begin to repair the relationships that have been compromised because of his gambling. He also understands that continuing to expose himself to situations where gambling is part of the picture might not be terribly effective; he isn't sure he has the self-control to bet a little when he has the urge to bet a lot and, although he might be able to dial back his activities for a while, he feels there's a real danger that he will slip into his old patterns before too long.

Gary realizes that in some ways, abstaining from gambling entirely might be the best course of action. He understands that this requires a strong sense of commitment. The tradeoff is that he'll remove himself entirely from situations and relationships where gambling is the driving force and probably give him the best chance of controlling the urge to gamble. Without gambling in his life, he'd have time to focus on his career; he could start jogging again like he used to do when he was younger. This plan isn't without risk, however. Gary might begin drinking again to fill the void, he could get bored and miss his gambling associates, or his anxiety might build up to such a point that he loses control and starts to gamble again anyway. Even if he succeeds, the myriad problems with his finances and strained relationships aren't going to disappear overnight.

Gary realizes that either course of action—moderation or abstinence—carries pros and cons. As you consider similar decisions, what do you believe is your best course of action? Write down the answers to these questions in your journal.

1. What will you gain by continuing to gamble, even if you cut back on how much you gamble right now?
2. Will you consider it a success if you succeed in cutting back your gambling? Would you gain more if you stopped gambling entirely?
3. There's a chance you won't succeed in moderating your gambling the first time you try. Are you willing to risk being unsuccessful? Can you afford to be unsuccessful?

4. Is there a possibility that you won't be able to abstain entirely from gambling at this time? Is that something you're willing to risk?
5. Do you want only a modest change to your current lifestyle, or do you want much larger changes?
6. Putting aside the question of moderation versus abstinence for the moment, do you have a plan of action if you should relapse to gambling? What is it?

Whatever you decide, it's important to understand that changing a behavior takes time. For many people, their biggest fear is that they won't be able to control the urge to gamble no matter what. It's true that whether you choose to slow down gambling or forgo it entirely, you could stumble several times before you get it right. Accept that setbacks are common among people who are in the midst of change. Even if you fail, you always can try again—and again and again. The more times you make an attempt to continue the journey toward recovery, the more likely you are to reach your destination.

MAKING CHANGES

Regardless of whether you make the choice to moderate or abstain completely from gambling, you can try to do so with self-help techniques, by seeking professional help, or by using some combination of the two approaches. You also have the option of making no attempt to change whatsoever.

We want you to consider all of the options for recovery from gambling so that you have a clear understanding of what each entails as well as the potential risks and rewards. There are advantages and disadvantages to each approach and the decision about which pathway to follow is likely to affect many areas of your life—your family and friends, work, mental and physical health, finances—not just gambling. Let's learn more about Gary's path and how the decisions he makes could affect him.

Making No Attempt to Change

Most people think that a gambling disorder is a progressive illness that always gets worse over time. Current research suggests otherwise: the general trend seems to be that the majority of gamblers move from excessive gambling to less gambling over time. One simple reason for this is that many people with gambling disorders eventually run out of money. Even so, there are no guarantees. Gary might struggle to control his gambling for many years if he doesn't take steps to get better, and the

> If you continue to chase gambling losses, you're very likely just to lose more money. In the end, the house always needs to make a profit to stay in business. The odds of winning are *never* in your favor. You don't have control over the event outcome, whether it's a game of chance or a game of skill.

same may be true of you. It's like most things in life: the more effort you put into controlling your gambling, the more effective your recovery is likely to be.

Gary understands that, in some ways, it would be easier to let things go on as they are. He wouldn't have to make any special effort or face the important problems in his life in a meaningful way—but there wouldn't be much payoff either. The likelihood of consequential improvements is much slimmer if he makes no effort to control his gambling. Despite the obvious drawbacks of doing nothing, Gary doesn't know whether he's ready to face the challenges of doing *something*.

Depending on your circumstances and thought process, you might not be ready to take control of your gambling just yet. Keep reading. Listen to how the techniques and strategies we suggest in the upcoming sections could affect Gary and how they might work for you. Just because you're not ready right now doesn't mean you'll never be ready. When you are, you'll have the information you need.

Attempting to Make Changes on Your Own

As he thinks about the consequences of things continuing as they are, Gary ultimately decides that it's time to try to get his gambling under control. He doesn't want to be in debt for the rest of his life, and he doesn't want to lose personal connections that are important to him. After some soul searching, Gary has decided that abstinence is the only path to recovery that makes sense for him. He believes that any exposure to gambling will ultimately lead to more gambling. The only way he will have any chance at a good life, he thinks, is to make his gambling a thing of the past.

Because he doesn't feel comfortable going to a therapist or attending group meetings at this time, Gary decides to try some self-help techniques first. He likes the idea of taking control of his own recovery. It won't be easy, but for the first time he feels determined to make the effort. He decides to start by taking some very basic, simple steps.

Recognizing Your Urges

Just because you make a decision to stop gambling doesn't mean the urges to gamble instantly disappear. They probably won't. Think about what happens when you feel an urge to gamble. Do you get anxious? Nervous? Do you quickly give in and act on the urge?

Here's a quick tip: flip to Chapter Five and Chapter Eight and try the relaxation techniques described. Relaxation is one of the most straightforward yet effective ways to help overcome urges.

We believe it's important to recognize and acknowledge that you are having an urge. Once you face this fact, ask yourself to wait ten minutes; it can help to set a timer to ensure that you wait out the full ten minutes. As you're waiting, focus on a distraction or get involved in an activity that interests you. It can be anything: Gary, for example, pulls out his iPod and listens to a customized playlist he put together specifically for this purpose.

At the end of ten minutes, if your urge to gamble has subsided, great. Go about the rest of your business. If your urge doesn't pass in the first ten minutes, reset your clock for another ten minutes and try another distraction. Gary takes a brisk walk or does exercises with an exercise band he keeps in his desk drawer; this has the additional benefit of helping him reach his goal of getting back into shape as he gives up gambling.

If the gambling urge still doesn't subside, try phoning, texting, or instant messaging a friend or family member you really trust and have him or her talk you through what you're feeling. It helps to enlist this person beforehand so that he or she expects to be engaged in this way. Having someone available who understands is one value of getting a sponsor through a self-help program. (For more on sponsors, see the section on support groups later in this chapter.)

You'll find that the gambling urges eventually pass. They always do. The trick is outlasting the urge whenever you can. The technique we've described here can help you do just that. It might not always work for you, but sometimes it will, so it's good to have such a simple tool for change in your toolbox.

Managing Your Finances

Not surprisingly, many people who have gambling problems are also in debt. In fact, few people who gamble ever win more than they lose. Paradoxically, increasing debt often motivates many gamblers to continue gambling. Gary always gambled even more when he lost big. He figured it was the only way he could make up for his losses and possibly even get out ahead. He was always wrong about that in the long run, even if it was sometimes true in the short term. He finally realized that he literally had a better chance of being struck by lightning than of hitting a lottery jackpot or getting rich from his gambling escapades.

To get out debt, you first need to take a good hard, honest look at the true state of your finances. This can be a very difficult thing to face, but it's a critically important step. We'll describe what Gary has done in this regard, but keep in mind that there are many methods for resolving your debt. You may want to enlist the help of an accountant or financial expert; they use more sophisticated tools than Gary decided to employ. Either way, the principle remains the same: your goal is to stop or curtail your gambling at least to the point that you are able to clear your debt.

Gary started by making a list of all of his outstanding bills and debts; these included his credit card balance, bills that were past due, and, of course, all of the loans from his brother. He used a chart similar to the one on the following page.

Once you've filled out your Financial Debt Chart, you will need to create a plan for paying back this debt. Look at this as a starting point. You can move forward from here one step at a time.

Gary doesn't have a wife or girlfriend or many close friends beyond his gambling circle. Despite all the problems gambling has caused him, he remains close to his brother. After filling out his Financial Debt Chart, he showed it to his brother, accepted responsibility for his actions and issues, and asked for his brother's continued support. This was tough to do; he respects his brother and wants his brother to respect him. After listening to what Gary had to say, his brother was elated. He not only pledged his support but also expressed relief that Gary was finally taking steps to get his life on track. In fact, this was the first thing Gary had done in a long time for which he did feel respect.

Gary agreed that his brother would be allowed to monitor his finances closely for at least the next year. Then, together they would reevaluate whether it was necessary to continue such an arrangement. This is a smart move. If you are trying to control gambling and get out of debt, you too should consider this sort of arrangement with someone you trust. It gives you another set of eyes to manage your ongoing finances and the pay-down of any money you owe; it also provides the opportunity for social support.

Financial Debt Chart

Use the following chart to list all of your outstanding debt. List to whom the debt is owed and the total amount you owe. Don't forget to factor in the interest rate, if any, as this can affect how quickly you'll be able to pay back the loan. List the minimum monthly payment; if the debt is to a friend or family member, discuss this amount and agree on an arrangement. Next, project how long it will take you to completely repay each debt.

At the bottom of the chart, list the total amount of all your debt combined as well as the total monthly dollar amount you will need to keep up with your payback program. It may help to put this on a spreadsheet that automatically calculates and updates totals.

Debt Owed to	Amount Owed	Interest Rate	Minimum Monthly Payment	Expected Length of Time It Will Take to Pay Off Debt
Total:				

However, you might not feel comfortable having a friend or family member oversee your finances. If this is the case, consider hiring a money manager, accountant, or debt management specialist. You also can use software or online solutions, but if you choose this route, you won't have someone else supporting your efforts.

With his brother's help, Gary prioritized his outstanding debts. Besides the money he owed his brother and his late rent and car payments, he had an outstanding balance on several of his credit cards; these required immediate attention because the interest was beginning to pile up. The brothers agreed that Gary's best strategy was to pay down his credit cards as quickly as possible while also meeting the minimum payments on his other debts. Gary believed that by putting in overtime at his job, he would be able to manage this plan.

To help get a handle on his spending habits and ensure that he could meet his monthly requirements, Gary and his brother also worked out a monthly spending budget for each of the next six months; they adjusted the budget for each particular month to reflect periodic and quarterly expenses. We've provided a sample budget worksheet like the one Gary used. Adjust the line items as needed, and fill it out as completely and honestly as you possibly can.

As Gary began to pay down his debt, he felt a lot less stressed out, and his self-image improved. He thought about how the stress of his debt often led him to step up his gambling for some relief. He now realized the folly of his actions.

Paying off what you owe may take a lot of time depending on the size of your debt, but don't get discouraged. If you follow your debt plan and use the suggested tips, you will reduce your debt. Remember to celebrate the smaller victories by doing something nice for yourself, such as giving yourself a spa treatment at home or cooking a great dinner or having a movie night with good friends. Just as you owe others, you owe yourself. This is hard work, and you deserve some fun.

Setting a Monthly Budget

Copy this monthly budgeting sheet into your journal or into financial software. Try to be as honest as possible and include all the areas in which you spend money in a typical month. You can use previous bank statements, credit card bills, and canceled checks to make sure you are as accurate as possible. Once you fill this out, track your expenses for the month to determine the accuracy of your original budget, and adjust accordingly. Fill out a unique budgeting sheet for each month to reflect seasonal and quarterly expenses. Consider using software or an online program that automatically tracks and updates dollar amounts.

Expense	Weekly Payment
Mortgage or rent	
Food and groceries	
Cigarettes/alcohol	
Debt (you will have calculated this amount in your Financial Debt Chart)	
Car—fuel costs	
Car insurance	
Telephone	
Utilities	
Work lunch costs	
Bus or train fares—work	
Parking	
Gambling (this will be zero unless your objective is to moderate rather than eliminate your gambling)	
Entertainment	
Seasonal expense	
Quarterly expense	
Other expense	
Total Monthly Costs	

Once you have a handle on your spending patterns, the next step is look for areas where you can save money and pay down your debt even faster.

All of us can identify expenses we can cut back on or remove entirely. Start by examining your four most costly expenses and think about how you can reduce them. Are these expenses luxuries or necessities? Do you need them, or do you want them? Then move on to the next four most expensive, and so on. It can help to save every single receipt for several weeks and keep a spending diary so that you can track where you spend your money to the penny.

As Gary poured over his budget sheets, he was able to see that he could save money by walking to work some days, by making his lunch instead of going out to a deli, and by making coffee at home instead of stopping for an expensive designer brew on the way to work. All these changes had the bonus of also being healthier. And more good news: because he had decided to abstain from gambling entirely, he was able to put a zero in the gambling column—a significant savings!

Identifying Your Triggers

People gamble for different reasons. Some do so to help deal with personal and professional stress. Others gamble only when they drink or take drugs. Some gamble in an attempt to make money, because the opportunity presents itself, or for emotional reasons—the list is endless. We believe that the primary reasons for gambling tend to fall into two categories: either as a distraction and entertainment or as a way to escape problems. If it's the former, you will find that you have some control over your actions at least some of the time; if your reasons tend to fall into the latter category, your gambling probably has a deeper, more personal meaning.

Think about the reasons you gamble and make a list of them in your journal. Keep in mind that you might gamble for one reason on some occasions and for other reasons on other occasions. Try to understand whether these triggers always cause you to gamble or just sometimes. You can have more than one gambling trigger, and some triggers are probably stronger than others.

As we mentioned before, it's difficult to say why Gary gambles. He would benefit from determining his triggers so that he could take steps to manage or avoid them. Once he gave his gambling triggers a good deal of thought and reviewed his entire history of gambling, Gary realized that he often gambles out of boredom. He could remember back in high school cutting classes to find a card game because he didn't feel stimulated by what he was learning. The same is now true of work. As the days go by and he sits in meeting after meeting bored out of his mind, his urge to gamble exponentially increases.

Gary also found that he likes the rush gambling gives him, especially when he's around other gamblers and when he's risked much more than he can afford. In fact, he's always found that the more he loses, the more he wants to gamble.

Knowing what your gambling triggers are and what needs gambling fulfills can help you identify substitute activities that don't result in similar personal and financial hardships.

Pre-Planning

You may sometimes be able to avoid the people you gamble with altogether. For example, you may only see them at certain bars or at the track; if this is the case, you can simply go to a different bar or stop going to the track. However, sometimes you're bound to see them no matter what you do, or because you want to continue to maintain the same friendships minus the gambling. For this reason, we believe that pre-planning is a topic that deserves special attention. If you can't completely avoid the people who tempt you to gamble, it's essential to have some avoidance and escape strategies in place to deal with these "human triggers."

Gary thought one of his biggest obstacles to overcome was the fact that most of his friends were also gamblers. Other than his brother, he felt little connection with anyone outside his gambling circle. Avoiding his gambling buddies depressed and isolated him, which upped his urge to gamble; at the same time, just being around these people left him vulnerable to temptation. What should he do?

If Gary still wanted to hang out with his friends who gamble, he could politely ask them not to gamble or even discuss gambling in front of him. Gary might also suggest a change of venue. For example, he could invite his friends to his house, where he can control the activities.

Obviously it can be very difficult to step away from well-worn habits and long-term friendships. However, this could be Gary's best course of action as he attempts to control his gambling. If you're in the same situation as Gary, we encourage you at the very least to let your friends know that you've decided to cut back or cut out gambling entirely. Sometimes the people you gamble with will not be as supportive of your recovery as you wish; sometimes they can surprise you and be more encouraging than you expect. You need to know where your friends stand on this issue and who can be helpful.

You also need to be prepared for people who, for their own selfish reasons, deliberately entice you to gamble. One effective method for dealing with these people is pre-planning your response. Take out your journal and make a list of all the people you know, separating them into two groups: people you associate with gambling and people you don't associate with gambling. The people you associate with gambling are the ones who are likely to put you in contact with gambling, spark the temptation to gamble, or deliberately push you to gamble. Next, brainstorm some strategies that can help you deal with your urges to gamble and help you avoid gambling when you're in the company of these people. Knowing your response ahead of time will help you follow through with it. You can use the Managing Risky Relationships worksheet as a guideline.

You can use the same sort of technique to help manage other triggers that also might lead you to gambling. For example, almost certainly there will be places associated with gambling that you won't be able to avoid. Beyond the bars and restaurants you typically go to, opportunities to gamble are more abundant than ever. You're likely to be exposed to gambling in places like delis, gas stations, and the Internet. There are now even smartphone applications that allow you to link your bank account directly to instant gambling Web sites, giving you the ability to gamble virtually anywhere at any time. Because it's nearly impossible to avoid all the people, places, and things that might trigger your gambling, pre-planning your responses can be an invaluable tool.

Managing Risky Relationships

Think of every relationship that puts you at risk and fill out the following chart. We'll use Gary as an example.

1. In the first column, write the name of a person with whom you have a risky relationship. It can be someone you gamble with or someone who intentionally or unintentionally tempts you to gamble. *Gary's friend Charlie calls him up several times a week and begs him to go to a poker game with him. Charlie doesn't have a car, so Gary is often his ride; Charlie really puts on the pressure.*

2. In the second column, write your typical "gambler's thought" in response to this person. This is the usual automatic thought that pops into your head whenever you are around this person or perhaps even thinking about him or her. *For Gary, his gambler's thought sounds something like this: "If I don't go, Charlie will be mad at me. He might trash talk me to others in the group. I should just go, have a good time and not rock the boat."*

3. In the third column, write a counterthought to the automatic gambler's thought. *Gary comes up with this counterthought: "I am avoiding all gambling right now, even if that means straining some relationships. I'm sorry if this hurts Charlie and he gets angry, but right now the most important thing for me to do is avoid gambling and work my way out of debt."*

4. Plan your avoidance strategy beforehand. There is no guarantee that it will work, but having a plan to deal with a risky relationship is better than being unprepared. *Gary will make other plans for as many nights of the week as he can so that when Charlie calls, he will have a legitimate reason for begging off on his invitation. He'll also go one step further and arrange for someone else to give Charlie a ride to the games.*

5. Record the outcome of your first few encounters with your risky relationship. This will help you determine what you can do better next time. If

your strategy works well, your success will give you the strength to persevere. *Things go well for Gary! Not only has he been able to resist his urges to gamble, but he's been spending more time at the gym and with his brother. Charlie is touched that Gary went out of his way to help him out, so he is more understanding than expected.*

Risky Relationship	Gambler's Thought	Counterthought	Strategy in the Moment	Outcome

Enrolling in Self-Exclusion

Gary has considered enrolling in his state's self-exclusion program. Many states, countries, and casinos have established self-exclusion programs that allow you to ban yourself voluntarily from entering casinos for a specified period of time—even up to a lifetime. If you go to the casino more than you want, find it difficult to leave the casino even when you've lost a lot of money, continue to gamble to try to win back your losses, or can't even drive past a casino without the urge to gamble arising, self-exclusion could be something to consider. Ask your friends and family about this. If they feel you have a major problem with gambling that centers around casino activities, this is another reason to consider registering with a self-exclusion program.

Self-exclusion programs do have limitations. Gambling providers, such as casinos, typically carry the burden of identifying and keeping out those who have excluded themselves. As a result, there is conceptual confusion with self-exclusion programs: individuals initiate enrollment, but gambling providers or jurisdictions manage them. Research indicates that self-exclusion programs result in some self-excluders entering casinos undetected, thereby breaching their contracts.

Attempting to Change with Professional Help

> Even if your gambling is severe, you can recover. The evidence shows that people with the full range of gambling problems can improve.

Gary's friend Valerie has attempted to stop gambling many times without much success. She's tried the same strategies that seem to be working so well for Gary, but none have worked for her so far. As much as she wants to stop gambling, it's been a struggle. Now she is in utter despair, and her financial and personal life are in ruins. Valerie knows that Gary is also in the process of managing his gambling and that he seems to be doing well.

Gary has been very supportive of Valerie. He's suggested that she keep on implementing self-help strategies; Gary also suggested that she consider professional guidance this time around. It's far from being a copout, he explains; there's no shame in asking for help if you truly need it. In fact, it's an incredibly brave thing to do.

Valerie isn't opposed to professional help; she's just scared. What if people find out she's seeing a therapist and attending group meetings? How can she share her deepest, darkest secrets with strangers? What if it doesn't help?

Gary has explained to her that no one has to find out about her treatment if she doesn't want them to. Therapists have an ethical responsibility to keep their patient's information confidential, and nearly all group therapy and support groups have a privacy code. No therapist, counselor, or support group member should judge her; they are there to offer encouragement, guidance, and strength. Gary and her family will certainly be there to cheer her on, but professional counselors have special training and resources most people don't have, and she would surely benefit from this. Gary points out that she'd get a fresh perspective on her problems and some new ideas for how to deal with them.

Although she's tight on time and cash, Valerie realizes she needs to view treatment as an investment, an investment that could potentially lead to far greater rewards than any slot machine jackpot. She's decided to start treatment as soon as possible. If, like Valerie, you've tried many times to control your gambling and used self-help techniques to no avail, treatment might be a good option for you too.

Support Groups

The first thing Valerie did was look for a local support group. She joined Gamblers Anonymous and began attending a local chapter's meetings just a few blocks from where she works. In those meetings, she listened to the stories of other members and discussed her own struggles with gambling; together with an experienced member, they worked through potential solutions and gave each other encouragement. This particular group followed many of the principles originated by Alcoholics Anonymous, such as the 12 steps and assigning sponsors to members who are still struggling with their gambling issues.

There are other programs that provide similar kinds of support, so if you decide to join a support group, do an Internet search to see what's available in your area. For example, if you want a program that supports your family members as well, consider Gam-Anon. You'll find more information about these groups in the Resources and Further Reading section.

One-to-One Therapy

Although Valerie finds her group meetings helpful, she also thinks she'd make more progress with some intensive, one-to-one therapy. Her Gamblers Anonymous sponsor has recommended a psychologist who specializes in treating people who are trying to control their gambling and also have other issues they'd like to address. Valerie thinks that working on her high anxiety levels and dealing with her frequent depression are an important part of her recovery from gambling. During her first session, her therapist explained that she can choose to tackle her problems with gambling alone or work on all her problems at once; both approaches are legitimate. The therapist emphasized that it's up to Valerie to create her own path. Valerie decided that it would be best to address all her problems at once; in fact, she believed that one of the reasons she'd failed to get her gambling under control in the past is that she had ignored these other problems.

In your own search for a therapist, a good place to start is with your primary care physician, clergy member, or human resources department at work. In addition, many states have public health or mental health programs devoted to gambling problems in the community; the specialists in these programs can put you in contact with clinicians who specialize in treating gambling problems. All of these are usually good sources for recommendations; you also can do an Internet search or ask someone you trust who has been through recovery. Besides psychologists, many psychiatrists, social workers, and trained counselors are equipped to help you get control over your gambling and the rest of your issues. If you don't click with your first treatment provider, that's OK. Keep looking until you find someone you trust and with whom you feel connected. It's worth the effort.

Residential Treatment

When she first started her therapy sessions, Valerie and her therapist explored the idea of entering a live-in residential treatment program. As her therapist explained, this can be a productive experience for individuals who have tried to stop gambling on their own many times or who have had a particularly destructive relationship with gambling. Residential treatment removes you from your life for a period of time; this is useful because it also temporarily removes your gambling triggers, allowing you to concentrate on the tasks associated with recovery. You work with trained professionals and attend groups with other people who are experiencing problems similar to your own. Although it's an idealized environment, some people find it necessary and useful to step back and take a breather. This experience gives them the opportunity to learn the skills they need so that they can carry them over into real, everyday life.

Valerie made the decision that entering a residential treatment wasn't the right choice for her at this time. She believes that the support of her friends and family, the daily group meetings, and the weekly sessions with her therapist are making enough of a difference; she wants to follow through on her current plan of action before considering such a significant change in course. That said, she is open to revisiting the idea in the future if she finds she isn't able to control her gambling with her current efforts; residential treatment is certainly an option for anyone who has tried hard to manage his gambling on his own but has not succeeded.

Medication

Another topic Valerie discussed at length with her therapist was the possibility of taking some sort of medication. There are various medications that have been used in research studies to help treat pathological gambling; these drugs hold the potential to help control gambling, but as of yet, there seems to be no instant cure-all. Treating pathological gambling with medication works much better in conjunction with other forms of treatment.

As her therapist explained, using medication to change gambling behavior requires a prescription from a licensed physician or psychiatrist. See Can a Medication Curb Your Urge to Gamble? for more details on this topic. If you consider any medication, discuss the potential side effects and drug interactions with your physician.

Valerie has decided to forgo taking any medication, at least right now. Similar to the decision she made about entering a residential treatment program, she feels she'd rather continue pursuing her current plan because it seems to be working so well. Wisely, she's agreed to keep the lines of communication open with her therapy team on the topic. Valerie is determined to change her life, so she is willing to keep all her options open.

CAN A MEDICATION CURB YOUR URGE TO GAMBLE?

Gambling affects your brain, just as drugs, alcohol, or any other psychoactive substance or activity does, by releasing "feel-good" chemicals that heighten the thrill of betting. Some scientists speculate that certain drugs currently used to treat mania and depression might also help dampen the urge to gamble.

One such drug, naltrexone, has shown promise in this area. Classed as an opioid antagonist, it seems to block the feelings of pleasure pathological gamblers get from gambling, so they simply lose interest in continuing. In one recent University of Minnesota study, 40 percent of patients given the drug quit gambling for at least one month. Their urge to gamble also significantly dropped in intensity and frequency. In contrast, the subjects who were given a placebo reduced their gambling by only about 10 percent.

Because medications work best in combination with therapy and other stop-gambling strategies, naltrexone and other drugs do not represent a *cure* for gambling, but they do seem to offer hope to many who are suffering from addiction. And although adding a medication regimen to help treat gambling disorders is a relatively new idea, emerging research is identifying new treatment options that make medications available to those who want to try them.

WHERE DO YOU GO FROM HERE?

You've been presented with some choices for changing your life and controlling your gambling. You now know that you can make a decision to leave things as they are, cut back your gambling, or give up gambling altogether. By following the stories of other gamblers, you've seen that you can attempt to control your gambling either with self-help techniques or with professional help. You've also learned that you can focus on only your gambling problems, or, if you've got other issues affecting your life, you can work on those at the same time.

After reading this chapter, you might be ready to start trying to manage your gambling with some of the strategies we've suggested. You might also be ready to start managing some of your other problems; if that's the case, we suggest moving on to one of the upcoming chapters that deal with problems that so often co-occur with gambling. Working on getting some of your other difficulties under control might help you manage your gambling more easily; doing so can certainly help you improve your life. If you're not ready to work on any of your issues now, including gambling, that's not to say you won't be ready in the future. Either way, you have the information you need to start down your own unique path to recovery.

5 Anxiety and Gambling

What you'll learn in this chapter: Do you often experience a sense of worry that doesn't seem rational? Do you feel frequent concern that you'll somehow lose control or that bad things are coming your way, but you don't know why? If so, you're probably experiencing symptoms of anxiety, or perhaps even what mental health professionals refer to as an *anxiety disorder*. In this chapter, we describe the symptoms of anxiety and discuss how problems with anxiety can influence your gambling. We also present possible solutions or pathways that can help you handle your anxiety issues, and describe the self-help tools and strategies you can use for managing anxiety on your own, especially as it relates to getting your gambling under control.

Everyone experiences some anxiety. This is normal, and anxiety is useful under some circumstances. It helps alert you to danger so that you respond accordingly. For example, if you go swimming in the ocean and spot a shark, feeling afraid and swimming to safety make good sense. This is a rational reaction to a specific object and situation where there's a very real possibility that something bad might happen.

It's also completely normal to feel nagging worry when there's little danger of physical harm but there might be other possible adverse consequences. You might, for instance, be concerned about failing a test if you don't understand the material very well, about being unable to pay your bills if you've been out of work for a while, or about botching a presentation at work if you didn't adequately prepare.

Although a certain amount of anxiety is inevitable, for many people, feeling anxious can become disruptive. It can become so overpowering that it limits how well you're able to function in day-to-day life. Feeling a bit nervous when your boss asks you to give a speech can actually work in your favor by pushing you to write down your talking points and practice in front of a mirror. But if the thought of standing in front of a conference room full of people sends you into such a panic that you start sweating, feel short of breath, and have trouble making it through the day, then the level of anxiety you experience isn't productive, and it's possible that you need to consider dealing with it so that you can get it under control.

TYPES OF ANXIETY

As you are about to learn, anxiety takes many forms and is in fact a common problem. Nearly 30 percent of people experience some type of anxiety disorder, the most intense form of anxiety, at some point during their lives. Only a trained professional can definitively diagnosis a "disorder," so if you think you might be suffering from one, it's best to make an appointment with a trained mental health professional, such as a psychiatrist, psychologist, or counselor, to receive a formal evaluation. However, you don't need to have a full-blown anxiety disorder for anxiety to disrupt your life—or to benefit from dealing with your anxiety-related issues.

Let's first discuss common anxiety-related problems and then move on to a discussion about the common pathways to recovery as well as the accompanying strategies.

Panic

Everyone experiences moments of panic, a sudden fear that dominates or replaces rational thinking entirely. For Laura, it's more than that. She'll be sitting at her desk when, seemingly out of nowhere, she's hit with an intense and overwhelming sense that something bad is about to happen, even though she isn't sure what. Intellectually she knows there is nothing wrong, and somewhere in the back of her mind she feels quite silly and wishes she could just calm down. But she can't. Her breathing becomes shallow and rapid, and she can feel her heart thumping in her chest almost as if it's inside her ears. Her mouth goes dry, the room starts spinning, and she feels as though she's about to suffocate. Eventually the feelings pass, but lately these episodes are coming on more and more frequently. Between attacks, she's filled with the dread of anticipation: Will the next one hit while she is on a crowded train? Out to dinner? Home alone?

Laura suffers from *panic disorder,* and the episodes she experiences are called panic attacks. Typically an attack lasts for about thirty minutes, and although medical problems during a panic attack are extremely rare, the experience is so unpleasant and powerful that it seems life threatening in the moment. After having a panic attack, many people fear the thought of having another one, and this further heightens their anxiety.

Laura thinks her difficulties with gambling are directly related to her level of anxiety. When her anxiety mounts, this is usually the time she has the strongest urges to gamble. Internet poker, in particular, seems to assuage her level of panic, if only for the time she's playing; focusing on the game distracts her from her inner feelings. But even then it can be difficult for her to completely escape her anxiety.

If Laura's experience sounds all too familiar, you might also suffer from panic disorder, and it might be affecting your level of gambling. For a diagnosis of panic disorder, you must experience unexpected attacks that are similar to Laura's; these attacks must include many of the symptoms listed here, without them having being brought on by a medication or medical condition. You must also have a persistent worry about having more attacks, worry so intense that you feel as though you're going crazy; you fear constantly that you are going to lose control.

SYMPTOMS OF PANIC DISORDER

- Shortness of breath or feeling as though you are suffocating or choking
- Rapid heartbeat; chest pain or discomfort
- Dizziness or feeling as though you are going to faint
- Trembling or shaking
- Sweating; hot and cold flashes
- Abdominal distress
- Intense fear of losing control or dying or going crazy, or that something bad is about to happen
- Feelings of unreality, as though you are not all there or are somehow observing the situation
- Numbness and tingling of the extremities

If you begin avoiding certain places because they seem to trigger panic attacks and you can't deal with the potential embarrassment this causes, you might suffer from what's known as *panic disorder with agoraphobia*. For example, you avoid going to the movies, not because the movies cause you anxiety, but because of an overwhelming fear that you might be unable to escape the embarrassment of having a panic attack as you sit in the theater.

Social Anxiety

Margret, an art student at the local college, is very talented and passionate about her work. But when it comes to asking questions in class, attending extracurricular activities, or interacting with like-minded classmates, she simply cannot bring herself to do it. Consequently, she skips a lot of classes for fear of being asked a question and completely avoids any contact with her fellow students. One of her instructors hopes Margret will present her paintings at an upcoming art show, an idea that sends Margret into an absolute tizzy. Whenever Margret feels her anxiety escalating, she turns to gambling, primarily online poker because it's anonymous and doesn't require real social interaction. Playing temporarily arrests Margret's fear that people will say nasty things about her work and put her down. However, it's an activity that drains her bank account too. She increasingly finds herself under financial stress, which ultimately magnifies her panic and low self-esteem.

A MYTH ABOUT SOCIAL ANXIETY

One myth you might tell yourself about social anxiety is, "I will not become anxious as long as I avoid situations, places, or thoughts that cause my anxiety." But the fact is that avoiding things tends to make anxiety worse in the long run because it makes the things that trigger anxiety even more frightening and worrisome. You might also start to avoid things that are even remotely related to your original source of anxiety; this will begin to limit how well you function in your everyday life. Unfortunately, most people have little practice working through this kind of anxiety. One way to think of it is that certain places, situations, people, or thoughts might make you uncomfortable; however, there was a time that these anxiety triggers were not unbearable. This means that the way you *respond* to these anxiety-provoking instances can add to the problem or even create new problems. Changing your response is an important step to getting better.

Do your thoughts and behavior mirror Margret's? Her marked and persistent fear of social situations and her panic at the thought of showing her work in public are classic symptoms of *social anxiety disorder.* If you suffer from social phobia, your dread of being humiliated or not knowing how to behave in public is so great that you avoid social situations as much as possible. You might have panic attacks at the mere thought of being exposed to a feared social situation, even though you recognize that these fears are unfounded and irrational. Your avoidance of socializing may have become so problematic that it now interferes with your normal routine and your ability to live your life. Like Margret, you might be using some form of gambling as a way of managing your discomfort.

Specific Phobias

A *phobia* is a strong fear and avoidance of a particular circumstance or thing. You can be phobic toward just about anything. Fear of snakes is a good example of a common phobia. Although many people would prefer to avoid being in a room with a snake, someone with a snake phobia finds the experience—or even the thought of it—intolerable. The snake could be a harmless garden snake or even a rubber model, but it doesn't matter; the fear is so ingrained and intense, it elicits a panic response.

Even if you understand that your phobia is irrational, you may not be able to control your reaction. In some cases, phobias can cause overwhelming distress. If a phobia is particularly severe and you begin avoiding any circumstance where there is even the slightest chance of encountering the trigger, it can have a troublesome effect on your life.

Generalized Anxiety Disorder

Everyone worries about something, but Rich is a *worrier*. From the moment he wakes up in the morning to the moment he goes to sleep at night, he worries about everything and nothing. He describes his thoughts as a worry loop because he seems to cycle endlessly through the same set of nagging worries over and over again. If you ask him what he's worried about, he can sometimes tell you, but just as often he can't quite put his finger on it, or the list is so long that it seems endless.

The only thing that seems to break his worry loop is betting on sporting events, especially horse racing. Placing bets helps distract him, albeit for a short time. Unfortunately, he tends to lose more than he wins, and whenever he loses, the thought of dwindling finances goes onto his long list of apprehensions and fears.

A persistent, unfocused, unending worry that carries on for more than six months is known as *generalized anxiety disorder (GAD)*. If, like Rich, you worry all the time but not about anything specific, this could be your problem. You may worry so much that it affects you physically; lately, Rich has begun to have migraines and backaches. You may have bouts of insomnia or difficulty concentrating, or feel irritable much of the time as the burden of worrying begins to wear you down. Having these problems also may contribute to your urges to gamble.

Post-Traumatic Stress Disorder

The events of September 11, 2001, were harrowing for all Americans, but significantly more so for the people who witnessed it firsthand. Patty is one of those people. She felt abject terror as the first plane hit the World Trade Center tower in downtown New York City just steps from her office. She was an eyewitness to the death and destruction that took place on that day. She was grateful to escape with little more than a few scratches and some smoke inhalation, especially considering that some of her coworkers and friends didn't make it.

At first, she thought she was moving past it. But one night toward the end of September 2001, she was sitting at a restaurant when a busboy behind her dropped a dish. Without thinking, she dove under the table, crying and shaking. A few days later, she was walking down the street and saw a plane flying overhead; she became so convinced it would crash into a building that she froze, unable to move. Often she was so upset that she couldn't go to work for days. She began having nightmares filled with planes spiraling out of control and bodies falling from buildings; during the day, she would frequently close her eyes and relive over and over again in her head what she'd seen. It got so bad that she wouldn't leave the house without a large knapsack full of survival supplies.

Never much of a gambler before, Patty now found herself obsessed with buying and scratching off tickets, which she did several times a day. It was one of the few activities that helped her feel better or even hopeful because she could dream of a different life. All of her symptoms, including the gambling, went on for years before she finally decided to get help.

Post-traumatic stress disorder (PTSD) is often associated with soldiers who have been in combat, but anyone who has gone through a terrifying, traumatic event can experience PTSD. Patty seems to be dealing with a classic case of PTSD. Besides the difficulties she describes, symptoms can include avoiding any circumstance where there is even a remote chance that the traumatic events might reoccur—even now, Patty avoids downtown New York. Just the thought of going there makes her heart pound and her palms sweat—and brings on a feeling of hypervigilance, a heightened state of watchful anticipation or being on guard, a sureness that danger is lurking around the next corner.

If you suffer from PTSD, you might notice, in addition to symptoms and experiences similar to Patty's, that although you're focused on the horrific event, you don't recall a lot of the details. Perhaps you've stopped socializing or participating in activities you used to enjoy, and you feel strangely detached from life. You might also be prone to sudden angry outbursts. You might have difficulty concentrating, calming yourself down, or planning for the future. Even if you never had an urge to gamble in the past, you do now, or, if you were gambling before, you gamble even more now and have difficulty keeping your gambling under control. This has lasted for some time since the event has occurred and might be escalating in intensity as time goes on.

Obsessive-Compulsive Disorder

Andrew is a classic example of someone who is overcome with anxiety much of the time. He started having anxious feelings when he was just seven. Even at that tender age, he would insist that the doors in the house be locked at all times to prevent a break-in, despite the fact that his family lived in a relatively safe area. He would even lock his bedroom door at night.

The older Andrew grew, the more his concerns increased, and often these worries centered on safety. When he left the house every day, he'd worry about the stove being left on and imagine that his mother was suffocating from the gas. He'd try to relax by telling himself that everything would be OK, but that didn't always work, so he would call his mother and ask her to check the stove, even though he knew he'd already checked it himself. Even then he would continue to obsess.

When Andrew was younger, he thought winning a lottery jackpot would ease his worries. So he started buying scratch cards, sometimes spending up to $50 per week while still in high school. As an adult, he is spending most of his free time playing casino games. The more he plays, the more he loses; the more he loses, the more he plays, trying to make up for his losses. He is stuck in a vicious cycle of anxiety, fear, worry, and gambling, making it ever more challenging for him to hold down his job and keep his family life together.

When, like Andrew, you are so obsessed with an anxiety-provoking thought that you feel the need to repeatedly perform a behavior to manage that anxiety, you are said to be suffering from *obsessive-compulsive disorder,* or OCD for short. You might realize on some level that your fears are somewhat irrational, yet cannot stop yourself from having those fears anyway. To limit obsessive anxiety, a person with OCD thinks or does irrational things over and over. Gambling is one possible compulsive activity. Other examples include washing one's hands many times a day, checking the door multiple times to make sure it's locked, or taking a certain number of steps to go to a certain place. It's common for such compulsions to take up much of the person's day—sometimes hours—and interfere with his or her daily routine. If you find yourself repeatedly thinking about something and then compulsively repeating a behavior pattern over a significant period of time, it's possible you are suffering from OCD.

THE ANXIETY-GAMBLING CONNECTION

Gambling and anxiety often go hand in hand. The 2001–2002 National Epidemiologic Survey on Alcohol and Related Conditions, as well as other recent research, suggests that among people with the most severe type of gambling problems—what mental health professionals label *pathological gambling*—more than 11 percent are dealing with a generalized anxiety disorder; almost 15 percent are suffering from PTSD; nearly 22 percent are dealing with a panic disorder; and 52 percent are struggling with a specific phobia.

Many people gamble as a way of managing anxiety. As they gamble, they often report being separated from their anxious feelings, or they project their feelings of anxiety onto the excitement they feel when they partake in their gambling activity of choice. As a result, gambling can work its way into the fabric of their everyday lives, and the impulse to gamble can overwhelm the rest of their lives.

Do you think any trouble you have with anxiety affects how much you gamble? Why? How so? How much? These might be tough issues for you to face, but let's try.

Answer as honestly as you can the following questions (in the "Is There a Connection . . ." box) about how your anxious feelings relate to your gambling; then carefully review your responses. This should be a very enlightening exercise. As with all the exercises in this book, consider writing your answers in a separate notebook so that you can keep all of your information in one place and can reuse these pages another time, perhaps after you've had a chance to work through some of the self-help strategies later on in this chapter and elsewhere in this book.

Is There a Connection Between How Much Anxiety You Feel and How Much You Gamble?

Think about the last few times you gambled and circle the underlined word that most closely describes how you felt:

1. Just *before* you have an interest or urge to gamble, are you <u>anxious</u> or <u>relaxed</u>?
2. *While* you have an interest or urge to gamble, are you <u>anxious</u> or <u>relaxed</u>?
3. *When* you decide to gamble, are you <u>anxious</u> or <u>relaxed</u>?
4. When you're anxious, do you gamble with <u>more</u> or <u>less</u> money?
5. Do you gamble for a <u>longer</u> or <u>shorter</u> amount of time when you're feeling anxious?
6. While you are gambling, are you <u>more</u> or <u>less</u> anxious?
7. Ten minutes after you're done gambling, are you <u>more</u> or <u>less</u> anxious? What about twelve hours after?

Now answer the rest of the questions here:

8. On a scale of 0 to 10, with 10 being extremely anxious and 0 being not at all anxious, how anxious are you when you win at gambling?
9. On the same scale, how anxious are you when you lose?
10. On the whole, do you think gambling could be making you more anxious?

    ☐ Yes   ☐ No

11. On the whole, do you think anxiety makes you gamble more?

    ☐ Yes   ☐ No

12. Have you altered your daily life to avoid feelings of anxiety?

    ☐ Yes   ☐ No

13. Do you sometimes fill these voids by gambling more?

    ☐ Yes   ☐ No

14. If you got your anxiety issues under control, do you think it would be easier to control your gambling?

    ☐ Yes   ☐ No

Despite its potential and real drawbacks, gambling can be one way to relieve the stress of anxiety. If you're limiting your social life or other activities as a result of anxiety, gambling might be how you fill the void that anxiety can leave. Anxiety can take a heavy toll on your life. Think about your favorite pastimes besides gambling, drinking, and substance abuse: When was the last time you did any of them? Even simple pleasures like folding clothes, taking a walk, or sitting in the garden become impossible when you feel overwhelmed by anxiety.

It's important to put gambling in perspective. Yes, it can help you keep anxiety at bay, but this is a temporary fix. It won't resolve any of your underlying issues in a permanent way. In fact, excessive gambling is more likely to lead to new and additional problems, including more anxiety, especially as it relates to finances and relationships. You are better off looking for a more meaningful path to change.

MAKING CHANGES

There are three main pathways to help manage your anxiety:

1. Make no attempt to change.
2. Attempt to make changes on your own.
3. Attempt to change with professional help.

Keep in mind that these pathways aren't mutually exclusive; you can choose what you like from each to create a unique course of change that works for you. You also should be aware that any pathway we describe can differ from your actual experience with it. The important thing to consider is which path is best for you at this moment.

Making No Attempt to Change

As with any major endeavor, deciding to overcome anxiety has its pros and cons. On the plus side, it will help you feel better and give you more free time to spend with your family and do the things you love.

On the minus side, all the changes you want to make might not come to you easily, leaving you feeling discouraged and disappointed. Before deciding which pathway to recovery you want to try, list in your journal at least five pros and five cons of trying to manage your level of anxiety, then answer the questions that follow.

1. Do the cons outweigh the pros?
2. Can you think of any ways to turn what you consider a con into a pro? For example, one of the cons of making this change is that it's very intimidating to tackle your problems. But imagine if you succeed. Your self-confidence will soar and give you the motivation to take on other big challenges in your life.
3. Can you imagine being successful and how that success will affect your life?
4. How would the pros and cons of trying to control your anxiety affect your urge to gamble and your gambling activities?

Consider Andrew, whom we met earlier in this chapter. Andrew, as you may recall, suffers from OCD and most likely has some other general issues with anxiety that cause problems in his life and lead him to spend a lot of his spare time and finances on lottery tickets, the track, and the casino. He's gotten to the point where gambling has eaten away his savings and now cuts into his weekly finances. His wife is threatening to leave if he doesn't get his act together. This makes him even more nervous, and he escalates his gambling to relieve the tension. And so it goes in a vicious cycle of anxiety-gambling-anxiety.

If Andrew decides to leave things as they are and do nothing about addressing either his anxiety or his gambling, this will certainly require the least amount of effort of all three potential pathways to recovery. And some research shows that it's possible, in time, that he might get better anyway. Among gamblers with severe problems, more than 49 percent improve annually; among gamblers with lesser problems, more than 54 percent show improvement at least one year later. However, things sometimes get worse before they get better.

If you are in a position similar to Andrew's, then you are faced with a similar challenge: tackling chronic anxiety can be a long, multistep process, and making changes can be difficult. However, one consequence of not managing your anxiety is that the intensity will ratchet upward. You might find that, like Andrew, the more you experience anxiety, the more you gamble, and the more you gamble, the more anxiety you experience. If this is the case, then perhaps leaving things as they are is not the best course of action for you. You owe it to yourself to keep reading to find out more about what potential solutions are available to you.

Attempting to Make Changes on Your Own

With his wife threatening to leave and his gambling losses mounting, Andrew understands the toll both anxiety and gambling have taken on his life. He knows he has to do something. After much soul searching, Andrew is finally considering making some changes, but he doesn't feel ready to seek professional help. He's decided to try some self-help strategies.

His biggest concern is that making changes in his life will require a lot of time and effort, and he's not sure he's up to the task. But he feels he has to try. Andrew thinks that, if he succeeds, he will transform his life.

There are a number of self-directed skills Andrew can work on that can make a tremendous difference in his anxiety level. There's also a good chance that these skills will significantly help him manage his gambling as well. There's also a good chance that these can help you too if you're willing to do the work.

Building on Past Success

As you ready yourself to make changes, it helps to recall a time when you have been able to achieve a major goal—a success of which you are really proud. To do this, we ask you to consider a previous major accomplishment in your life. How did you achieve it? What motivated you to succeed? What were the obstacles you needed to overcome to reach your goal? In the following exercise, you'll answer questions and write down information that will help you retrace your steps on the path to this previous success.

1.   Write down a brief description of a past accomplishment. It can be anything that makes you feel proud, such as a promotion at work, winning a community service award, or teaching your child to read. If it made you feel good about yourself, then consider it a success.

2.   In the following chart, list the challenges you faced and all the skills you needed to successfully deal with those challenges; then list the responses you used to overcome those challenges. For example, getting a promotion at work might have involved mastering a new software program that was difficult to learn; perhaps you spent some nights and weekends studying the manuals and practicing the skills. But doing all that extra work was worth it because it paid off.

Challenges	Skills	Responses to Challenges

3.   What motivated you to succeed? Was it the promotion itself, more money, or the satisfaction of acquiring new skills?

At first you might not think that winning a promotion at work or teaching your child to read has a lot in common with tackling anxiety or gambling. But it's just as important to learn from your successes as it is to learn from your mistakes. Your accomplishments in life probably required a good deal of your time, effort, and attention. Although you might not draw on all of the same abilities you've used in the past, you might be surprised to learn how many of these same qualities and resources are likely to come in handy for the task at hand.

As you get started down the path toward recovery, think about what this will mean for you. How do you think your journey will unfold? What is motivating you to move toward recovery, and especially, what is pushing you toward directing the process on your own? What obstacles do you think you will encounter, and how will you deal with them? Do you think you can be successful, and if so, what does success look like in your eyes?

You have the ability to succeed. Just look at your responses to the exercise here. Consider rewriting these exercises using anxiety and gambling as the example so that you can see what skills you have or need to develop and how you might manage these challenges as successfully as others you have dealt with.

Learning to Relax

One of the most powerful ways to counteract anxiety is by learning to relax. It isn't possible to be relaxed and anxious at the same time. Relaxing means more than simply plopping yourself in front of a TV or surfing the Internet. Real relaxation is a physiological and psychological response that is the opposite of anxiety and panic. It's accompanied by a slowing of the heart rate and lowering blood pressure, deeper breathing, and a calm, even state of mind. When experienced on a regular basis, the effects of relaxation are cumulative.

If your level of anxiety is so high that it makes you physically and psychologically uncomfortable, taking active steps to relax yourself can offer relief. Relaxation exercises, such as the ones we've outlined in this section, teach you to identify worry triggers, diffuse them, and break the cycle of anxiety. We recommend you commit to daily practice, even if the exercises don't appear to help you at first; the more you do them, the more positive effect they will have.

Being able to relax is a skill, and as is true of any other skill you want to develop, you will improve with practice. The more you practice, the more you'll become aware of the ebb and flow of your anxiety, and as soon as you feel its presence, you can target it. There are dozens of "mind-body" practices, such as yoga, tai chi, and meditation, that blend deep breathing and relaxation strategies with body awareness techniques that help you recognize when your body is too tense. Many of these are ongoing practices you can try at your health club or at a specialty studio, but fortunately you don't absolutely need to take a class to learn the basics of relaxation. It helps to understand which relaxation exercises are the most effective. So use an anxiety journal, like the one described next, to see which relaxation exercises work best for you.

However, before you learn to relax, it is helpful to get a handle on what is making you anxious in the first place. Greater awareness can help you anticipate these feelings, which in turn allows you to recognize the need to employ a relaxation strategy. For you to learn about your anxiety, we recommend that you keep an anxiety journal for at least one week. In it, record your anxiety level every hour or so, writing down what makes you anxious and what your thoughts and responses are to that anxiety. Consider rating your anxiety on a scale of 0 to 10, where 0 is completely relaxed and 10 is highly anxious. If you forget to make an entry during an hour, just skip it and move on to the next one; going back and trying to remember how you felt is not usually very accurate. After a week of tracking your anxiety, analyze your responses to see if you can determine any clear patterns. You might also consider writing in your journal again from time to time during your recovery to see how your anxiety (and gambling) patterns are evolving.

Here are two excellent relaxation exercises to get you started. You should avoid trying these during an actual panic attack because you might get confused and not realize when the attack has passed. You should also try to avoid doing these exercises right after eating, when your body is focused on the task of digesting your food.

Progressive Muscle Relaxation

The purpose of this exercise is to learn body awareness and the difference between tense muscles and relaxed ones. By slowly tensing and relaxing each muscle group in your body, you can teach yourself the difference between a relaxed muscle and a tense one. Once you learn this skill, you'll have a better sense of body awareness in situations that make you tense. With practice, you'll learn to cope with tension by training your muscles to relax and your mind to calm itself. As we said, it is not possible to be tense and relaxed at the same time. However, please note: intentionally tensing muscles isn't recommended for anyone with high blood pressure and certain other medical conditions or injuries. You should consult with your doctor if you have any disease or condition (for example, a bad back) that might be adversely affected by tensing muscles.

Set aside fifteen uninterrupted minutes. Find a quiet, distraction-free location. Dim the lights if you like. Sit or lie down in a comfortable position. To do this exercise, you will tighten each of the body areas listed here in succession. You'll focus your attention on one area at a time, tightening the muscles in that area to your point of comfort, usually about 70 to 75 percent of maximum effort. Don't overdo it, and remember to keep breathing.

Hold and squeeze each area for fifteen seconds (about ten slow counts), feeling the tension build up. Then release the tension and completely relax, allowing the tension to flow out of that area and away from your body. *Important: For every muscle group, take a moment to notice how different it feels when it's tensed compared to when it's relaxed.* Do one to three repetitions per body area before moving on to the next.

Move through the body areas in the order they are listed in the following guide. As you relax an area, give yourself a cue by either thinking or saying the word "relax." This will help you associate relaxation with one word, and this idea will start to carry over into your daily life when you are feeling tense and anxious.

For your hands, arms, feet, and legs, do this exercise on the right side first. When you are done with the entire sequence, move through the whole progression again doing the exercise on your left side. You will do centralized areas such as the shoulders and abdomen twice.

- Hand: Squeeze it into a fist and then relax it.
- Front of upper arm: Tighten all the muscles in the front of your upper arm and then release them.
- Back of upper arm: Tighten all the muscles in the back of your upper arm and then release them.
- Upper shoulders and neck: Raise both of your shoulders and tense up your neck, then drop your shoulders and release the muscles.
- Forehead: Raise your eyebrows and wrinkle your forehead, then lower the eyebrows and relax your forehead.
- Jaw: Clench then release.
- Cheeks: Make a forced smile, then relax it.
- Abdomen: Tighten your belly and lower back muscles, then relax them.
- Upper leg: Stiffen and straighten the muscles of your thigh, then relax them. If you are sitting, you will have to straighten your leg and lift it slightly off the floor; if you are lying down, you can simply squeeze and tighten the muscles to create tension. Keep your legs straight for the next two progressions.

- Lower leg: Tighten your lower leg muscles (shin) by pointing your toes to the ceiling, then relax your foot and muscles.
- Foot: Curl your toes and tighten the muscles in the bottom of your foot, then uncurl your toes and relax the muscles.

Diaphragmatic Breathing

Slowly exhaling sends your body and brain signals that help them relax. Practicing this type of deep breathing can help you breathe this way even when you're not actively engaged in this type of exercise.

Set aside ten uninterrupted minutes for this exercise. Find a quiet, distraction-free location. Dim the lights if you like. Sit or lie down in a comfortable position.

Place one hand gently on your chest and one hand on your abdomen, just above your belly button. Inhale deeply through your nose or through pursed lips for one slow count. Your lower hand will move out as your belly and rib cage expand; your upper hand should not move at all. Now exhale completely through your mouth for one slow count; your bottom hand should move inward as you feel your belly and ribcage grow smaller once again. As you exhale, think the word "relax." Your goal should be to breathe evenly and deeply rather than taking short, choppy breaths, which often accompany anxiety and distress.

Rest briefly, then repeat this breathing pattern, this time holding the inhale and exhale for two slow counts. Continue increasing each "repetition" by one slow count until you reach ten.

Tracking Your Progress

You might notice a big difference in your anxiety level after doing either of these exercises the first few times—but you might not. As we mentioned, relaxation is a skill that takes practice. Try doing at least one of the relaxation exercises twice daily, and you will begin to get better at it within a couple of weeks. You probably will also find that these exercises teach you skills that help you manage your feelings of anxiety and gambling urges at other times too. If neither of them seems to work for you, try adjusting your position, adding some visualization (see box), or changing your practice to a different time of day.

VISUALIZATION

You can add visualization to virtually any exercise in this chapter or use it on its own as a technique for minimizing anxiety. A classic visualization exercise is to imagine a safe, peaceful place or situation, using all five senses to conjure up as much detail about it as possible. This helps draw your attention away from tense negative thoughts and urges. For example, imagine taking a leisurely walk on the beach. You see the ocean, sun, sand, and birds; you hear the waves crashing against the shore, and the wind blowing as the birds call to each other; you feel the warm sun on your skin and the soft sand beneath your feet; you smell and taste the salty air . . .

Tuning in to your body and environment helps bring your visualizations to life. The more detail you can conjure up, the more "real" your visualizations will seem and the more relevant they will be to helping you tune in and diffuse your anxiety level.

- Be aware of your five senses
- Be aware of your body
- Be aware of your breathing
- Be aware of your emotions
- Keep thoughts in the here and now

Finding Replacement Activities for Anxiety

One of the best ways to relieve anxiety and minimize urges to gamble is to do something else, an alternative activity that is positive and enjoyable. This helps take your mind off issues you tend to worry about. Finding a replacement activity means taking up old hobbies or finding new interests and activities. This provides you with coping mechanisms to effectively manage anxiety and gambling.

Think of at least five activities you enjoy doing that have nothing to do with gambling, drinking, or substance use. For instance, you might enjoy watching TV, working out, or gardening. The key to this exercise is to find activities that work best for you. In your journal, fill in a chart like the one shown here to help you clarify what activities you like to do, how much time you like to spend doing each activity, and what aspects of each activity make you feel relaxed. Whenever you feel anxious, consider revisiting this list and engaging in one of the activities until you feel less anxious.

Activity You Enjoy	Amount of Effort Required (very little, moderate, or a great deal)	How It Helps You Relax When You Are Anxious

Reprogramming Automatic Thoughts

Your thoughts and the way you interpret what happens in your life profoundly affect your emotional state and your behavior—which in turn profoundly affect your thoughts and interpretations. When your thoughts are frequent and automatic as well as negative and counterproductive, they can begin to interfere with your life. Learning how to identify these so-called automatic negative thoughts (ANTs) and how they can affect your level of anxiety and your propensity to gamble is essential to helping you manage them.

It might surprise you to know that learning to tolerate some uncertainty is one of the keys to banishing ANTs and managing anxiety. ANTs are so definite in their interpretation of events that they give you a perpetual sense of impending disaster. Rational responses offer alternative scenarios. So, rather than feeling that things definitely will end badly, open yourself to the possibility that they could end well. This doesn't mean that you should lie to yourself or tell yourself everything will be OK when this simply isn't true or you don't know for sure. In some instances, you do bear responsibility for the outcome; telling yourself otherwise would be counterproductive.

Changing ANTs is a two-step process. First, you must recognize your most frequent ANTs; second, try substituting alternative, rational thoughts for the negative ones. (Review the list of types of ANTs on the following page to see if you can identify the ones you experience most often.) With practice, you can gradually transform your ANTs and reactions into more useful responses. The next exercise can help you identify, interpret, and replace ANTs. Try it, and you'll be surprised at how many ANTs pop into your head over the course of a day. Come back to this exercise from time to time to track improvement.

EXAMPLES OF AUTOMATIC NEGATIVE THOUGHTS

Overgeneralization: drawing a conclusion based on a single event; expecting something that happened once to always happen

Filtering: focusing on the negative and ignoring the positive

All or nothing: thinking in extremes, with no middle ground

Personalizing: thinking that everything is a reaction to you

Catastrophizing: overestimating the likelihood of disaster

Emotionalizing: mistaking feelings for facts; believing that negative things about you must be true because they feel true

Mind reading: making assumptions about other people's thoughts, feelings, and behaviors without considering evidence

Fortune-telling: expecting a certain outcome and assuming that your prediction is a fact

"Should" statements: using "should" or "must" statements that create unrealistic expectations for yourself and others

Magnification and minimization: tendency to exaggerate the importance of negative information and minimize the worth of positive experiences

Record your ANTs throughout an entire day, including the situations in which they occur, how they affect your behavior, and how anxious they make you feel. Evaluate each ANT and describe the specific evidence that supports your underlying assumptions for why each might be true and the specific evidence that it may be false. Does analyzing your ANTs in this way make them seem more or less rational? Can you think of more rational responses?

Situation	ANT	Effect on Behavior	Anxiety Level (0–10)	Why the ANT Is True	Why the ANT Is False

Exposure

Exposure is a technique whereby you face your fears in a planned and controlled setting; this allows you to build up a tolerance to anxiety and become accustomed to situations and thoughts that provoke it. It can be difficult to face your fears in this manner, but if you can push past them, exposure can be a very effective way to deal with your issues. In our experience, managed exposure is a particularly useful technique for people who suffer from OCD, panic disorder, social anxiety, general phobias, or PTSD.

To practice exposure, start by using your relaxation skills to get comfortable. Once you are relaxed, you gradually introduce thoughts about the object, place, or circumstance that makes you anxious. Once you are comfortable with this task, you gradually increase your exposure by first viewing pictures of whatever is causing you anxiety. Then, once you can tolerate viewing pictures, you step up the exposure by placing yourself in the same general area as the source of the anxiety. Once you can tolerate this, you step up the exposure again by moving closer and closer to the source of anxiety until it no longer causes fear or worry.

Recall our example of the person who has a snake phobia. Once relaxed, he can start by closing his eyes and picturing a location where he saw a snake. If he can maintain his feelings of relaxation while experiencing this mental picture, he can move on to looking at a picture of a harmless snake and then perhaps standing in a room where a snake in a terrarium is placed a considerable distance away. All the while, he must maintain his state of relaxation. If all goes well, he gradually can move closer and closer to the snake; perhaps one day he'll even be able to hold the snake without feeling extreme anxiety.

Repeated exposures are most effective, so frequent practice without exceeding the limits of your comfort zone work best. You don't want your anxiety level to rise so high that you aren't able to continue. But if your anxiety level ratchets up too far during an exposure, it's perfectly OK to take a break and just relax. It can help to set a time limit on exposures and give yourself time between sessions so that you can gather yourself and prepare for another round.

Never place yourself in a situation that is dangerous or potentially life threatening. For example, if you're afraid of germs, it's fine to touch a garbage can but not biohazards, such as used needles or raw sewage. Exposures are designed to teach you to cope with your anxiety in a controlled yet safe manner—so make sure you set yourself up to succeed.

The example of the anxiety curve illustrates how exposure to fear of freeway driving begins with a manageable level of stress that gradually increases until anxiety reaches a tolerable level. Once that happens, you might find it useful to do some rational thinking where you replace your ANTs with more reasonable thoughts to help deal with the remaining anxiety. This type of rational thinking will help you manage fear both during and after the exposure.

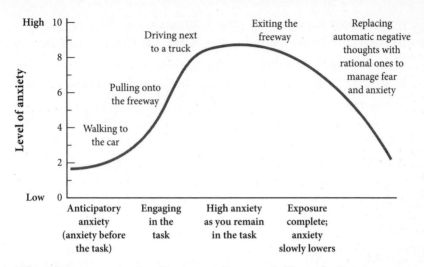

What Happens to Anxiety During an Exposure? (Example: Driving on a Freeway)

Remember, anxiety and relaxation are incompatible. In addition to this type of rational thinking, use the relaxation breathing and muscle relaxation techniques you've learned as well.

Exposure helps you to confront the things that make you anxious and to think in new and different ways. For example, during an exposure, you don't tell yourself that everything will definitely be OK when you don't know for sure that's the case; you also don't tell yourself that something terrible definitely will happen when that's not necessarily the case either.

Once you complete an exposure, don't undo all the good. It's not uncommon to feel some anxiety immediately afterward. If you do, sit with your anxiety until it dissipates and keep in mind that you only experience anxiety for limited periods of time. Use your relaxation skills. Stay in the moment and let your worries melt away on their own. Anxiety always passes. Always.

We don't advise beginning with the most anxiety-provoking circumstance in your life. Think of anxiety as a ladder with the least scary thing as the bottom rung; start there. What is one thing you fear that, when you are exposed to it, puts your anxiety at less than a 6 on a 10-point scale where 0 is not at all anxious and 10 is the most anxiety you can possibly imagine? Be very specific. This lesser fear is easier to tolerate than your biggest fears, but is still somewhat anxiety provoking.

Use the chart to enter when, how many times, and for how long you would like to work on exposing yourself to this fear during the next week. You can adjust the number of times you practice a task based on how quickly or slowly you develop a tolerance to the situation.

	Task	Time	Check Off Once Completed
Day 1			
Day 2			
Day 3			
Day 4			
Day 5			
Day 6			
Day 7			

HOW TO THINK BEFORE, DURING, AND AFTER AN EXPOSURE

- Practice relaxation exercises before and after an exposure. If an exposure becomes too intense, consider stopping to do some relaxation work before continuing with the exercise.
- Review rational responses before, during, and after the exposure. Identify ANTs and substitute rational alternatives.
- During the start of an exposure, visualize yourself facing your fears calmly and rationally; rehearse the thoughts and actions you plan to think and do during the exposure.
- While doing an exposure, try to stay in the moment. Don't focus on what happened before you started or what will happen once you're done.

Preventing Avoidance

One of the most common anxiety-related behaviors is avoidance—avoidance of material things, social situations, or particular thoughts and feelings. You might gamble, drink, or use substances to help avoid thinking about or doing something, but these activities offer only temporary relief from worry.

When you avoid the things that encourage anxiety, those triggers begin to loom larger in your mind and gradually can become even more frightening and worrisome. You might also start avoiding other things that are somehow related to the original thing you are trying to avoid in the first place—then your anxiety really begins to snowball. Avoidance reinforces the belief that there is something to be worried about, even if that belief is irrational.

Part of learning to control your anxiety is changing your relatively automatic behavioral reactions to anxiety, including avoidance. This chapter has given you some useful new tools—such as relaxation exercises, replacement activities, and counterthoughts to ANTs—that can be very powerful in helping you face anxiety head-on. If you employ these techniques, you can minimize the chances of inadvertently encouraging more anxiety.

Use the following table to write down how you will work with some of the new tools in this chapter to replace your usual avoidance strategies when you are feeling anxiety.

Situation or Thing Avoided	Usual Avoidance Strategy	New Tool to Manage Anxiety

Attempting to Change with Professional Help

Although self-help will work for some people, you might not be able to get past your anxiety on your own. Even if you aren't diagnosed with an "anxiety disorder," you can still benefit from getting professional help. A professional clinician can help guide your change even as you continue to use the techniques you learn in this book.

After years of struggling with lack of sleep and chronic nervousness related to PTSD, Patty, whom we discussed earlier in the chapter, ultimately decided to seek help. This finally allowed her to face her years-long struggle and get on with her life. At first she was hesitant about seeking help: she figured that she had enough friends and family around her that she should be able to deal with her problems by herself. But her therapist explained to her that although it's always good to have the support of loved ones, they don't always have the training or wherewithal to provide the kind of help she needed. And it's true: professional counselors, clinicians, and medical doctors spend years learning about problems, suffering, and how to change behavior patterns. They possess the skills and resources to help you; usually these skills are more advanced than those your family and friends have to offer. This doesn't mean that you don't need assistance from family and friends; it just means you might need more help than they can give you.

It took Patty a while to build up trust in her therapist, who was, after all, a complete stranger. Her therapist reminded Patty during their first session that she was legally bound to keep everything in their sessions confidential. Patty soon found it refreshing to hear objective advice and opinions from someone with a different perspective. She stopped letting her fear of being judged be a concern and began focusing on her recovery. She still used a lot of the self-help tools we've outlined in the book—with the therapist's encouragement—and this helped her manage much of the anxiety she'd been experiencing since 9/11.

One last note about Patty's journey: early in the process, Patty and her therapist discussed medication, which can be a good course of action for some people who experience anxiety. For example, in one clinical study led by researchers at the University of Pennsylvania Medical Center, more than 40 percent of patients who took the selective serotonin reuptake inhibitor (SSRI) paroxetine for GAD no longer experienced significant symptoms by the end of an eight-week trial. However, Patty opted to go the therapy-only route, keeping an open mind about exploring the idea of medication if her anxiety didn't improve within a reasonable amount of time.

MYTHS ABOUT ANTIANXIETY MEDICATION

You might have heard that antianxiety medication is very dangerous and can cause addiction. The fact is that if prescribed by a doctor and taken correctly, benzodiazepines, the most common type of antianxiety medications, can reduce anxiety effectively. This drug class includes alprazolam (Xanax) and lorazepam (Ativan). However, taking too much can impair your ability to operate a motor vehicle or other equipment. Drinking while taking these medications is also dangerous and can cause a variety of serious problems. Some people who use benzodiazepines become dependent on them, but using the lowest effective dose for as short a time as possible reduces this risk. Talk with your doctor about these and other risks associated with benzodiazepines and other medications. Remember, misusing any medication can be dangerous, so be certain that you understand the medication and its proper use.

Another myth about antianxiety medications is that their use automatically will lead to weight gain. In fact, most medications prescribed for anxiety don't seem to be associated with weight gain. However, tricyclic antidepressants, which are used occasionally to treat anxiety, *have* been associated with weight gain.

Like Patty, you might decide that you could use some support. Or perhaps you've been trying the self-help pathway and you either haven't been as successful as you'd hoped or feel that you could benefit from some professional help as well. Whatever you decide, try not to allow the fear of being judged by a professional, your loved ones, or anyone else factor into your decision. As we stress over and over again throughout this book, mental health problems—much like physical problems—are not a sign of weakness. Anxiety disorders can affect your functioning, your quality of life, and your physical health. Millions of people have benefited from getting professional help. Help from a professional can take a variety of forms, including individual, family, or group treatment. The only people who need to know about your journey are the ones you want to have know about it. You *deserve* to feel better.

WHERE DO YOU GO FROM HERE?

Now that you've reviewed the information about all three pathways, including extensive information about the self-help strategies you can try right now on your own, do you have a sense of what will work best to help get your anxiety under control? We hope this chapter has helped you see that there are ways to deal with your anxiety and that doing so can also help you manage your gambling. But maybe you're not yet ready to address your anxiety issues. You don't have to feel rushed to make a decision. If you aren't ready to make changes right now, it doesn't mean you'll never be interested in change. Most likely you will be at some point. After all, people change all the time.

If you do decide to try making changes now, you might discover that at times you lapse back to your previous ways of thinking and acting. If you do, don't become discouraged. Be proud that you've taken the first steps toward recovery; if you've made it this far, you've already accomplished a lot! When you do experience a setback, pick up where you left off, but examine what led to the lapse. Review your experiences, thoughts, and feelings before, during, and after a period of anxiety. Repeat the exercises in this chapter to help reaffirm your anxiety triggers and the strategies that bring you the most relief.

Remember: it's normal to be concerned about what the future will bring. We're confident that by putting in the effort, you can gain more control over your anxiety and your gambling.

6 Mood Disorders and Gambling

What you'll learn in this chapter: If your moods have become increasingly difficult to handle or you feel that moodiness and emotions contribute to why and when you gamble, this chapter has significant information for you. It describes common problems with moods and helps you decide if perhaps you have a full-blown mood disorder. We help you explore all the possible options for managing moods, including self-directed strategies that can help you get both your moods and gambling under control.

Moods are the way you feel over time. These feelings influence and reflect the way you experience the world around you. Experiencing and expressing your emotions through moods is one way you connect with other people and react to events and circumstances.

People have different reactions to similar events. You might think that everyone reacts to the exact same things in precisely the same ways; this isn't so. People who like water parks will feel excited and happy when they visit one, but people who consider them dirty, overpriced, and noisy can feel irritated and grumpy at the mere thought of a water park. And of course, your moods fluctuate all the time. Perhaps you start your day at a water park in high spirits, but as the lines grow longer and your feet get tired, you begin to feel progressively more annoyed.

A mood disorder is a sustained, prolonged mood disturbance, such that your moods and emotions begin to intrude on and restrict your life. Typically people with mood issues struggle with just one or two emotions rather than a wide range of them; sadness and pleasure are two emotions in particular that commonly cause problems. More than thirty million Americans a year suffer with some sort of mood issue. But you don't need a clinical diagnosis for moods to be a disruptive force in your life—or to do something about them.

TYPES OF MOOD PROBLEMS

To begin addressing your moods and emotional state, we'll start off by defining some typical problems. See if you recognize yourself in any of these descriptions. Next we'll move on to some strategies and solutions, focusing particularly on self-directed techniques and those that also can have the greatest impact helping you manage your gambling.

Depression

When Jamie was in nursing school, she used to play poker with her roommates once a week. She won some; she lost some. Either way, she liked playing cards so much that, when she graduated, she continued gambling on a regular basis. After Jamie started working at the children's hospital, she'd hit the nearby resort casinos every weekend.

Normal sadness lasts for a few days. Depression can cause suffering for years if you don't deal with it. Constant hopelessness and dejection do not have to be part of your life.

At this point, she still had things under control; she always set a spending limit and never exceeded it. She met a wonderful man who joined her at the tables most weekends. They fell in love and got married.

Within a year, Jamie's new husband grew tired of wasting so much time and money. He wanted to start saving for a home and family. Jamie tried to respect his wishes—what he wanted seemed so reasonable, and she wanted those things too—but when she tried to stop card playing cold turkey, she missed the flashing lights of the casinos, the feel of the chips in her hands, her poker buddies—and the thrill of the risk most of all. Soon she was sneaking off to gamble on her way home from work. At first it was just a couple of times a week for a quick game, but before long, she was gambling several hours a day, every day, spending way past her limit and going to elaborate lengths to cover her tracks. Not surprisingly, she and her husband began to drift apart.

Jamie buried herself under a mountain of lies—and a mountain of debt. It didn't take long for her husband to discover her stash of gambling money and betting slips. He confronted her and told her that if she didn't stop gambling, he'd leave. When it was clear that Jamie's gambling wasn't going to slow down, her husband made good on his promise and moved out.

Now she's heartbroken and feels completely alone. Jamie finds herself crying a lot these days. She's lost interest in her job as a pediatric nurse, her family, her friends—her life, really. She has chronic insomnia, yet she has trouble dragging herself out of bed most mornings. She's barely eaten in a month, and as a result, she's dropped nearly twenty pounds. She used to go to the gym a couple times a week, but no more. Now she spends most of free time crying and watching TV. Her job—a job she loves—is in jeopardy because she simply can't focus on the basics like filling out paperwork and showing up on time. Her world is crumbling, but she's in such a deep funk that she can't seem to pull herself together.

We all have moments of sadness. But what Jamie is experiencing goes far beyond a case of the ordinary blues. Clinicians describe her state of mind as a *depressive episode* or *major depressive disorder (MDD)* if it isn't followed by a period of high energy and extreme enthusiasm, or *mania* (more about mania shortly).

Depression is defined by feelings of sadness so profound that you feel hopeless, angry, and sometimes so sluggish that it seems as if you can barely move. And you can feel this way for days, weeks, months, or even years at a time.

When you're depressed, you experience, as Jamie has, changes in your sleep and eating habits. You might lose interest in activities you normally enjoy, and find yourself crying a lot. Feeling this way can affect your ability to get through the day and to function properly at work, school, and home.

Do these symptoms sound familiar? If you feel depressed on most days during a two-year period or longer but don't experience a true depressive episode with symptoms as magnified as Jamie's, you might be living with *dysthymia,* a disorder that is similar to MDD but not as severe. Either way, if depression is somehow coloring your life a dull shade of gray, you may want to address it.

Mania

Brian sometimes goes through stretches of emotional highs where suddenly sleep feels optional and life is great. He springs out of bed each morning full of excitement, his creative juices flowing, his confidence soaring. Several days into one of his recent energetic moods, he decided to landscape his yard. His lack of experience, skills, and tools for such a project didn't put a damper on his enthusiasm. He started by pulling up all the bushes around the house—with his bare hands. From there, he dug up flower beds, churned up the lawn, yanked out fence posts, and attempted a paint job on the porch, with disastrous results.

Mania is *not* the same as feeling great. Even though mania is sometimes described as extreme elation, individuals with mania often do dangerous, impulsive things that can have serious adverse consequences.

During this time of great energy, Brian also started placing huge, impulsive bets on football games and other sporting events. He was flying so high that he felt invincible. Even as he lost tremendous amounts of money, he was confident that his next big win was just one bet away and his losses would be wiped out in an instant.

That's not how it happened. He bet and lost thousands of dollars; he destroyed thousands of dollars' worth of property. Finally, his brothers, coowners of the property, convinced him to stop landscaping—and to stop gambling. It took weeks of repairs and several expensive contractors to put things right. Worse, his brothers had to dip into their savings to cover Brian's gambling debts.

At first, Brian's exuberance probably seemed positive to those around him, but it quickly became apparent that he was becoming more outlandish, and his behavior was more out of control by the day. Mental health professionals call this cluster of symptoms and behaviors a *manic episode*.

If you've experienced some of the same symptoms and they've lasted longer than four days, mania might be an issue for you too. Here's what to watch for: instead of feeling down, you're filled with energy and enthusiasm for days or even weeks on end. During this time, your thoughts might be filled with plans for the future, and you have the feeling that nothing can stop you. Just like Brian, you might start out with an inflated sense of self-confidence, which can lead to riskier decisions and increasingly more grandiose and impulsive behavior as your episode progresses. You might not rip up the lawn, but you might go on a spending spree, engage in indiscriminant sex, drink excessively, or gamble more than usual.

Manic episodes often begin as an upward shift in mood; you feel happier, more vigorous, and better able to concentrate. At first, you're probably more productive than normal. In the early stages, you might feel euphoric and sleep less, either staying up much longer or waking up several hours earlier than usual. As the episode advances, you might experience what is sometimes referred to as "flights of ideas" as your thoughts begin to race so quickly that you feel as if they are about to take wing. You might have a compulsive need to talk for hours; in the most severe form of mania, your speech may become incoherent. During a very intense episode, you might even start to hallucinate.

Bipolar Disorder and Cyclothymic Disorder

Although it's true that highs and lows are all a part of life, the severe mood swings of bipolar disorder can include aggressive, dangerous behaviors and unbearable misery—and they are not something you need to live with.

Inevitably Brian's manic episodes come to a screeching halt, and he crashes into numbing depressions. For Brian, this process isn't gradual; it usually happens rapidly.

When someone has unpredictable moods that swing wildly from depression to mania, we often suspect a diagnosis of *bipolar disorder.* However, this is a challenging diagnosis to make because of the wide range of emotions everyone experiences and the wide range of normal reactions to what's going on in a person's life. Typically, if a person's mood swings are so radical that it becomes difficult for him to act normally and his behavior becomes disruptive to those around him, we consider a bipolar diagnosis a strong possibility.

If your moods tend to vary to the point that they interfere with how you live your life but perhaps not to the extent associated with bipolar disorder, then it's possible that you are living with *cyclothymic disorder,* which is similar to bipolar disorder, but less severe. Symptoms of cyclothymic disorder include, on the mania side, insomnia, distractibility, and a persistent irritable or elevated mood for four consecutive days or more. On the depression side, symptoms include a loss of interest in almost all activities and a persistent depressed, sad, or hopeless mood for more than two consecutive weeks.

GAMBLING AND MOOD

Even if you didn't experience intense moods before you started gambling, you might now, because of the effect excessive gambling has had on your personal, professional, and financial life. Mood issues and problem gambling often go hand in hand. The 2006 National Epidemiologic Survey on Alcohol and Related Conditions found that about 20 percent of the population qualifies for a mood disorder at some point in their lives, but among problem gamblers, it spikes to more than 50 percent.

Jamie is a good example of someone whose issues with gambling and mood are intertwined. The only thing that gives her any relief is the very thing that helped make her life such a mess in the first place: gambling. For some people, it's the other way around: they gamble because they are already depressed. But either way, depression and gambling often coexist in a vicious cycle that can be difficult to break.

Is There a Connection Between Your Mood Swings and How Much You Gamble?

Think carefully about the last few times you gambled, and write down your answers to the following questions.

1. When do you do most of your gambling?
2. How do you usually feel before you gamble?
3. What is your mood typically like while you are gambling?
4. Does winning at gambling usually change your mood? How so?
5. How do you feel after you've gambled? Does it depend on whether you won or lost money?
6. Now that you know more about the signs and symptoms of mood problems, do you think it's possible that your moods and gambling are linked in some way? If so, how?

Looking back, Jamie realizes not only that gambling has contributed to her depression but also that she's probably used it to manage her moodiness for a long time. When she was in school, she'd play cards to deal with a bad grade or a fight with a friend; when she first started work, it was her way of coping with the sadness she felt at caring for so many sick children; during her marriage, she'd head off to the casino rather than confront her husband with any potential conflicts.

Gambling and mania have a clear and very dangerous association as well. Because someone in the midst of a manic episode can experience delusions of grandeur, when he gambles he is likely to take far greater risks than he would when he is thinking clearly.

Whatever the case, the rush that often comes with gambling can serve as an escape from overwhelming emotions. If you have extreme highs or lows, even if you haven't been clinically diagnosed with a mood disorder, addressing only your issues with gambling won't help you make lasting improvements or lead to a more satisfying life. You'll need to deal with your emotional peaks and valleys in order to make real progress and feel better about yourself.

MAKING CHANGES

There are three main options, or pathways, for facing your issues with mood:

1. Make no attempt to change.
2. Attempt to make changes on your own.
3. Attempt to change with professional help.

As with any issue you face, you can use any of these solutions exclusively, or you can try a mix-and-match approach. The more severe the disorder, the more we urge you to seek professional help. What really matters is coming up with a plan that works for you and that yields the best results.

Making No Attempt to Change

If you decide you aren't ready to make any changes right now, you won't need to expend any extra effort—but there probably won't be much payoff either. Think about Brian for a moment. If he allows things to continue as they are, how many more times will he destroy thousands of dollars' worth of property? When will he damage one of his relationships beyond repair? How many more times will he descend into the depths of depression that inevitably follow his episodes of manic euphoria? When, if ever, will he decide that enough is enough?

If you have mood swings, even if they aren't anywhere near as intense as Brian's, they probably will continue to cause you difficulties if you don't address them, and, as a result, the consequences might become increasingly troublesome and frequent. However, it's also true that mood swings may actually improve over time on their own; some people do find that their issues with mood—and gambling—eventually ease up even if they don't take any proactive steps toward recovery.

But it's worth asking yourself how much moods and emotions are truly affecting your life on a daily basis. Are they are holding you back from enjoying yourself and reaching your goals? Don't you owe it to yourself to be proactive about taking control of your moods and gambling?

Attempting to Make Changes on Your Own

Perhaps you're ready to make some healthy, positive changes in your life as they relate to your moods and gambling, but you aren't keen on working with a mental health clinician or attending group therapy. In that case, self-directed change may be a good option for you. Self-directed change or self-help means that you take the reins of your own recovery; you guide your own treatment without help from a professional.

Jamie, for instance, is considering tackling depression and gambling on her own. She's intimidated by how daunting this idea seems, and she's especially afraid to give up gambling right now because it's her only crutch, the one thing that offers her any sort of release from the crushing loneliness and depression she's been feeling since she separated from her husband. At the same time, she's at the end of her rope; she's in debt and in danger of losing a job she loves. With nothing to lose and everything to gain, she figures why not at least try some self-help techniques.

The strategies and techniques we outline in this section are geared toward directing your own recovery from mood issues. The approaches we suggest focus on replacing gambling with other activities as you work toward stabilizing your moods. If at any point you don't meet your goals, try not to get discouraged. One way to stay motivated is to choose goals that are meaningful and manageable and to set realistic expectations. We talk in depth about this topic in Chapter Three.

Reprogramming Automatic Thoughts

As we described in the previous chapter, thoughts, emotions, and behaviors all form a loop, and the characteristics of each have a direct influence on one another. Normally this is not an issue, but if your thoughts regularly lean toward the extremes and are frequent and repetitive, they can become problematic, especially when you're dealing with mood issues. We call these *automatic thoughts*.

Your thoughts are often a clue to why you feel the way you do. Thoughts can be colored by words (*I felt fat in my dress, so I didn't enjoy the wedding*), images (a mental picture of how terrible you looked in the dress), or memories (a memory of having trouble zipping up the dress and then looking in the mirror). By identifying your automatic thoughts, you can usually make better sense of your moods.

During a manic phase, Brian's thoughts tend to become overly optimistic and energetic; during a depressed phase, his thoughts are quite pessimistic and glum. Both ends of the spectrum have a profound effect on his everyday emotions and behavior. He's not likely to attempt another dramatic home improvement project while he's down—but he's not likely to have enough energy to mow the lawn either.

The first step to dealing with mood swings like Brian's is learning to identify your thought patterns so that you become more aware of them. Once you identify these patterns, you can come up with strategies to replace the problematic ways of thinking with different and more useful thinking. Being able to see your behavior with some perspective after the fact can help you better plan for those times when your mood is not very steady.

In this next exercise ("Tracking Your Thoughts and Moods"), we ask you to plot your moods on a day when you are particularly emotional, to help you determine any patterns that emerge. Even if you've done a similar exercise in a previous chapter, we encourage you to repeat it here as a way to help reinforce how your issues with moods might be affecting your thoughts and behavior. You should consider doing this for an entire week so that your emotional patterns are more likely to be revealed.

Once you identify your automatic thoughts, you can begin to challenge them and perhaps replace them with more rational thoughts. This is not always easy, especially when you're experiencing strong emotions like fear, anger, sadness, depression, or arousal. However, once you can learn to reframe your thoughts about a particular circumstance, you can begin to gain control over the moods associated with those thoughts.

For example, like most people, Brian is inclined to consider his beliefs as facts. Once, during a depressive phase, one of his brothers took him out to dinner, and Brian's thoughts involuntarily spun toward the negative: *He's only taking me out because he has to . . . He isn't enjoying himself . . . He wouldn't even talk to me if he weren't my brother . . .*

Gaining new perspective can help you change these types of thoughts. For this reason, it's useful to consider the accuracy of each automatic thought that runs through your mind, to see if there is any evidence to support it. By doing so, you open yourself up to new, potentially more constructive thoughts.

Tracking Your Thoughts and Moods

Every hour, note your mood and record it in your journal. Write down exactly what you are experiencing at the moment you write—what you are doing, what you are thinking, and how the thought makes you feel. Make a real effort to record the thoughts associated with the moods you are experiencing.

Date and Hour	Situation	Automatic Thought	Mood

Consider your thought-mood loops from the exercise you just completed. Focusing on some of the more problematic ones, ask yourself the following questions:

1. What evidence, if any, supported my automatic thoughts?
2. What evidence, if any, did not support my automatic thoughts? In other words, were there other ways to interpret the situation?

3. If it turns out that my original assessment of the situation was correct, was the situation really as bad or good as it seemed at first? What is the worst thing that could happen?

Considering these simple questions each time an automatic thought pops into your head might dramatically change your view of the world and the way you respond to circumstances throughout the day.

Finally, in your effort to manage your thoughts and moods more effectively, it helps to have options—that is, different thoughts that have the potential to take the place of those automatic thoughts, which are irrational and unfounded. Taking one or two of your more problematic automatic thoughts, try to come up with substitute thoughts and then consider how thinking differently is likely to change how you feel and respond to the situation.

Automatic Thought	Substitute Thought	New and Different Thought's Effect on Mood

To be sure, identifying and changing seemingly ingrained involuntary thoughts takes a lot of practice. Until you break the cycle of automatic thoughts, you might consider reviewing this section on a daily basis, filling out the chart in your journal and continuing your dissection of your automatic thoughts—from the most commonplace to the most negative and troublesome.

Identifying and Rating Behaviors

Just as thoughts are a clue to your moods, your moods are a clue to the way you think and behave. When you have trouble managing moods and emotions, they can drive you to engage in unhealthy activities like drinking and gambling, or keep you from engaging in healthy activities like exercising and spending time with your friends and family.

Transforming the way you think can have a tremendous impact on your mood and, in turn, your behavior. The opposite is also true: changing your behavior can have an incredible impact on your thoughts and emotions. Remember: thoughts, emotions, and actions are all links in the same chain, so by pulling on one, you influence the others. One very powerful self-help technique for changing moods and emotions is to change your actions.

Jamie, for example, now understands how strongly her gambling and moods are connected. She knows that by altering her pattern of gambling, she might feel less depressed and more in control of her life. She is thinking about limiting her casino trips to the weekends and setting spending limits as she used to, but this seems like such a huge undertaking. How would she even begin?

Much as she would edit her automatic thoughts, she can become more aware of her behavior and the specific moods attached to her actions. In the next exercise, we ask you to do exactly that: use your monitoring skills to observe your behavior patterns and then determine which behaviors require change based on the moods they elicit.

To do this, record your activities every hour on the hour for an entire day; briefly describe each activity you engage in, the associated mood or moods, and the intensity of the moods you feel at the time. To rate the intensity of your moods, think of a scale from 0 to 10, where 0 is not intense at all and 10 is as intense as you have ever experienced. Mild sadness, for example, might rate 3 on the scale, whereas powerful feelings of depression would rate 8, 9, or 10.

Remember, moods reflect emotions. So if it helps, rate the emotions that drive your moods. Give as accurate a description of your experience and associated emotions as possible. Although you're specifically focusing on the relationship between actions and emotions, here it also might help to note which automatic thoughts also enter into the loop as well.

Day and Hour	Activity	Mood or Emotion	Mood Intensity Rating

With the help of this record, you can identify which parts of the day you tended to be, for example, most and least happy, and what you were doing at those times. This can be a very enlightening exercise. Jamie assumed that the highlight of her day was gambling, but her real-time record surprised her by revealing that she actually felt quite lonely and sad as she sat at the card table. This revelation is helping her change her gambling. She now realizes that just as we can draw inaccurate conclusions about other people, we can be poor observers of ourselves.

This exercise allows you to determine which daily activities are candidates for change. If you find it especially useful or you note a strong link between a particular activity and mood, continue recording your behavior and associated moods for a week or so.

Creating a Schedule

Shaping your daily life with a tight and exact schedule, at least for a period of time, can do wonders for helping you manage your mood and control your gambling. You may be skeptical about this because you feel that you already have a schedule—for work, meals, and all the other aspects of your day. However, scheduling activities in advance and following your schedule can make a real difference by bringing clarity and structure to your life. A schedule can keep someone like Jamie from blowing off work, friends, and family to gamble instead of facing her problems; it can help someone like Brian when he is on one of his "highs" to stop making several appointments at the same time.

When you commit to a preplanned schedule, approaching your daily activities becomes simpler and less anxiety provoking because you know what to expect. And sticking to a set schedule can help you avoid spending uncomfortable time alone or resist the spontaneous temptation to gamble or engage in other unhealthy habits.

There are three different approaches to scheduling you can try. Depending on your particular issues, one might work better for you than the others.

Basic Scheduling

The easiest way to structure a schedule is to sit down every evening and prepare a detailed plan for the following day. As you create your schedule, include the approximate time of each task or event; leave a space to record your moods and emotions and the intensity levels of each. This process will allow you to think logically about the best way to organize your day, maximize your productivity, and minimize your stress. It also will help you focus on essential responsibilities on your to-do list.

Sample Schedule Page

Use the format of this sample to create your daily schedule. This is just an example, so feel free to edit it in a way that works for you, or buy one of your own. There are many paper and booklet-type schedulers readily available and easy to use. There also are many excellent cell phone and desktop scheduling applications. Whatever tool you use, we'd like you to schedule at least a week's worth of activities to start, so make sure it has the capacity to hold at least that much information. If you find this method helpful, consider using it for an extended period of time. Following is a snapshot of what a typical scheduled workday looks like for Jamie. As she went about her day, she filled in her mood and its intensity level, and used the Notes column for any other thoughts she had. She'll use this information to refine her schedule in the coming days.

(continued)

Day and Date: Tuesday, May 15				
Time	Activity	Mood	Mood Intensity Level	Notes
7:00 AM	Breakfast, check emails	Depressed	6	Feeling lonely; having some urges to gamble
7:30 AM	Exercise: Walk "Rolling Meadows" loop	Calm	5	Exercise helps
8:15 AM	Shower, change, head for work	Calm	5	
9:00 AM	Morning staff meeting/ assignments	Depressed/ anxious	7	A lot to do today— feeling overwhelmed
9:45 AM	Paper work/ patients	Depressed/ anxious	4	
12:30 PM	Lunch break with Christine	Excited	6	Nice to catch up with a friend and have some company!
1:30 PM	Paperwork/ patients	Anxious	5	Still trying to catch up
4:30 PM	Shift change meeting/ handover	Anxious	5	Some disagreements with incoming shift—did not finish work
5:15 PM	Drive home/ grocery shopping	Depressed/ anxious	6	Lonely cooking for one—resisting urge to gamble
6:30 PM	Make/eat dinner	Depressed/ anxious	6	
8:00 PM	Call Pia	Excited	6	Nice to have someone to talk with—helps gambling urges
8:30 PM	Watch TV	Bored/ worried	8	Feels like the time of the day that is most risky for me
9:30 PM	Read	Calm	3	
10:15 PM	Lights out			

Selective Scheduling

Another way to create a formal daily schedule is called *selective scheduling*. This involves reviewing your self-monitoring records to pinpoint what you do and how you feel about what you do. Reviewing the records you create allows you to consider planning your day to avoid places where you gamble or circumstances that you know tend to blow your moods out of proportion. Planning activities won't change your underlying feelings, but by scheduling relaxing and entertaining activities in advance that reduce your chances of getting stressed out, you can significantly reduce the likelihood that your symptoms will overwhelm you.

It's possible that you experience your most uncomfortable feelings while participating in required activities, such as work. Obviously, you can't typically schedule a bike ride with a friend or coffee with your book club during work hours. Still, there often are ways to organize your time at work so that you feel more comfortable and less moody. For example, it might be possible to plan to work on a project for an hour or so and then to take a ten-minute break to go for a walk and clear your head. If you don't have that kind of freedom, then consider using your lunch or break time to get out and move around or do something else you enjoy that's healthy and productive.

As you selectively schedule, remember to keep monitoring your activities and emotions. By continuing this exercise, you'll be able to determine which scheduled activities help you feel better and which don't do much to help you manage either your moods or your gambling. You can continue to revise your schedule and compare your emotional ratings day to day and week to week so that you can track improvement. Feeling different and having tangible evidence of this change will give you confidence that you're on the right path to making important life changes.

To start a selective schedule, first review your self-monitoring records from the earlier automatic thoughts and behavior exercises and highlight the activities that you feel are associated with your most problematic moods, thoughts, and behaviors. Then ask yourself the following questions: *Do I notice a pattern? Do I see specific times of day or particular activities where I feel particularly low or overexcited?*

Using the patterns you've isolated, plan the upcoming week, scheduling such activities as social engagements, events, and phone calls specifically during the times when you have particularly strong emotions or when you have a tendency to give in to the temptation to gamble.

Pleasurable Activity Scheduling

On the depression end of the mood spectrum, there is an inability to derive pleasure from activities that you once enjoyed, and when you feel incapable of enjoyment, you rarely have the energy to participate. On the mania end of the mood spectrum, you are focused on seeking exciting and stimulating activities, often regardless of the consequences. This arousal often feels enjoyable—particularly when compared to feelings of depression.

If you are currently in the midst of a manic phase, then scheduling pleasurable activities is typically not an issue. Someone struggling with mania is better off relying on self-monitoring records and selective scheduling to change his or her behavior. During a manic phase, you would be wise to seek out the support of close friends and family to help get protection from getting into risky situations.

If, however, you are in the throes of a depressive episode, you can benefit from scheduling pleasurable activities. A pleasurable activity can be anything you enjoy, from eating your favorite foods to window shopping to taking a trip. Even if you think that you have too many responsibilities or you think it's frivolous to find the time for recreation and fun, these activities can help lift your mood. Taking time for you, away from obligations and worries, is essential. It's absolutely necessary to stop once in a while, look around, and take a deep breath; doing something fun that brings you small pleasure and even great joy can be the deep breath that rejuvenates you.

If you are depressed, sad, or lonely, it's hard to imagine enjoying yourself or even giving yourself permission to enjoy yourself. You might be hesitant about scheduling something that makes you feel good, but pushing yourself to have a little fun or recreation can help change the way you feel. Who knows? You could discover a new hobby or reacquaint yourself with an old one. If one of your activities turns out to be less pleasurable than you anticipated, try something different next time. Enjoyable activities can help you avoid gambling by giving you a different way to manage your time and emotions.

As with any other type of scheduling, it's important to record your emotions during your scheduled "fun time." Having such a record provides valuable information you can use to evaluate what's working for you and what isn't; you can use this information to tweak your schedule going forward. And if it works and you start feeling better, you'll have the blueprint for success written in your journal for future reference. This next exercise will help remind you about activities that you enjoy and help you plan for them in your life.

Identifying Pleasurable Activities

1. List at least five activities that used to make you feel pleasure, joy, delight, or amusement but no longer do, or for which you no longer seem to have the time.
2. If you felt differently about yourself now, what activities besides gambling, drinking, or taking drugs would you enjoy doing?
3. Is there any activity you've always wanted to try but have avoided doing because of your moodiness or because you spend too much time gambling?
4. Imagine yourself engaging in any or all of these activities you've listed. Would you enjoy doing them?

Attempting to Change with Professional Help

If you try the self-help approach but feel it isn't enough or that you want more support than your friends and family can offer, consider seeking the advice of a qualified mental health professional. You can opt for individual therapy or group meetings specifically designed for people who want to conquer their mood issues; therapy can be focused on dealing with both mood and gambling. You also can seek out 12-step groups like Gamblers Anonymous, Bettors Anonymous, or Debtors Anonymous to get help with your gambling problems. Many people have found these groups essential to their recovery. At 12-step meetings, participants share their personal stories with other problem gamblers, and allow other members to discuss potential solutions. Together, they support each other as they try to control or abstain from gambling. Gam-Anon also uses the group meeting structure to provide support for the families of those suffering with a gambling problem.

Seeking professional help doesn't mean relinquishing responsibility for your recovery. On the contrary, going this route requires a significant commitment on your part; it also has great potential for reward. There are many advantages to having an experienced, qualified professional on your side: besides the years of education and training they're required to go through, having an impartial yet invested party to help guide you through the process of recovery can make all the difference.

Brian, for example, turned out to be an excellent candidate for professional help. Contrary to what he believed, his mood issues weren't always a response to something going on in his life; they were the result of a chemical imbalance in his brain. For this reason, his psychiatrist prescribed lithium for his manic episodes (only certain professionals can prescribe medication), and this seems to help him quite a bit. Lithium is a drug that acts on the central nervous system, and although it's not precisely known how it works, it does seem to help improve the coping abilities of people who struggle with mania.

There are often side effects with lithium that some patients find uncomfortable, so it is definitely not for everyone, as most prescribing clinicians would agree.

For Brian's depressive episodes, the doctor is considering trying him on a low dose of Prozac, Paxil, or Zoloft. All these drugs belong to a class of antidepressants known as selective serotonin reuptake inhibitors (SSRIs). SSRIs seem to alleviate the symptoms of depression by blocking the reabsorption of serotonin, a chemical in the brain associated with happiness and positive moods.

Besides taking medication, Brian is now attending one-on-one counseling and group therapy on a regular basis and employing some of the self-help strategies we outlined in the previous section. He's doing much better. His moods are stable for longer periods of time, and he's largely calmer and more even-tempered. This is a huge relief to his family. And, of course, it's easier for him to get on with his life.

Whether or not you decide to take medication is a personal choice and one that you should discuss at length with your mental health professional. Whether you choose medication or not, you'll probably have the most success with any approach to professional treatment if you attend regular meetings with your therapist or a group (or both) so that you get into a rhythm and stay focused on making changes. Regular treatment contact keeps you motivated and goal oriented. If you run up against obstacles or you relapse, your support system is already firmly in place. You also might find it useful to show your treatment professional any work you've done on your own—including anything you've done with this book—so that he or she will have a better understanding of the challenges you face and the strategies you're already using or have already tried.

WHERE DO YOU GO FROM HERE?

Recognizing the need for change and choosing the path to recovery that's right for you is a critical first step even if it doesn't solve all your problems right away. The process of recovery affects your whole life, not just your emotional state and your gambling, so although you might not succeed in reaching all your goals immediately, you move closer to recovery simply by *trying*.

Deciding you want to make a change is a victory in and of itself. Keep trying, even if you've failed in the past. Changing is a journey, and failed attempts to change still move you down the path toward recovery. It's quite possible that this time around you'll be able to make positive, lasting improvements to your emotional state and your gambling, and you'll do this with the help of self-directed strategies that are within your control.

7 Impulse Control and Gambling

What you'll learn in this chapter: In this chapter, we describe the signs and symptoms of impulse control disorders (ICDs), suggest ways to think about these urges, and explain how these problems can affect gambling. We discuss the different options for changing how you manage impulses, with an emphasis on self-help techniques. You'll find ways of dealing with ICD in general as well as some advice about dealing with specific forms of this problem.

An *urge* or *impulse* is the result of the tension that comes from simultaneously wanting to act and trying to restrain yourself. You experience the tension that comes from an intense sense of arousal; this stimulation derives from wanting both to resist and to act on the urge.

Almost everyone acts impulsively sometimes. Whether you take a spur-of-the-moment vacation, splurge on an expensive cell phone, or order a decadent dessert, following through on an impulse can be exhilarating so long as you can live with the consequences. Impulsivity becomes a problem when your urges start to have a negative effect on

Even if a doctor has not given you a diagnosis of an impulse control disorder, the information in this chapter can prove useful to your overall well-being—and it can help you change your gambling behavior.

you and those around you—and when you feel you must follow through with the impulse to release tension and experience a sense of gratification.

Impulse control issues appear quite common for people with gambling problems. More than 40 percent of people with gambling addiction also struggle with some aspect of ICD. In fact, difficulties with impulse control can cause the urge to gamble. For some, gambling is a way to act on an impulse. For others, gambling helps them forget about other impulses or helps make these other impulses feel less intense. Some individuals start gambling before they experience problems with impulse control. For this group, gambling probably leads to unintended consequences that adversely affect their health, relationships, and financial well-being; these consequences can lead to other impulse control problems.

No matter what leads you to gamble, the rush from gambling might serve as an escape from uncomfortable impulsive feelings. If so, dealing only with gambling problems is not sufficient. It will be important to identify and change the primary cause of your gambling, which might be impulsivity, depression, a combination of these issues, or something else entirely.

Perhaps you wonder if it would be easier to live with an ICD than to try to deal with it. Impulsive behaviors can remain enjoyable during the time you're not thinking about the range of potential consequences; gambling is more fun when you don't entertain the possibility of losing. However, this temporary pleasure doesn't solve more enduring problems. Although gambling can be a fun distraction, it doesn't help you resolve important problems. That's why it's so important to question whether the positive effects of your impulsivity outweigh the negative ones.

DIFFERENT FORMS OF IMPULSE CONTROL PROBLEMS

An ICD might seem like addiction because of the repetitive pattern of behavior; it also might resemble obsessive-compulsive disorder (OCD). Addiction, OCD, and ICD cause sufferers to struggle with impulse control. For example, as we discussed in Chapter Five, people with OCD repeat specific patterns of behavior; people with ICD, in contrast, discharge their impulses toward many different targets—for example, gambling, drinking, shopping, sex, and so on. People with ICD and OCD typically try to avoid acting on their impulses, only to experience an increasing strength in the impulses to act until they finally do act. People with addiction are different from those with ICD or OCD because they don't usually make an attempt to avoid their impulses; they act out their addictive behavior pattern and then typically feel bad about their intemperance afterwards.

Some people are impulsive about only one thing; others are all over the map. Some behave impulsively in a variety of ways; others repeat the same specific behavioral patterns over and over again. To gain a sense of the larger scope of problems that loss of impulse control can cause, let's meet some people who struggle with common forms of ICD.

Hair Pulling and Skin Picking

Rosa is going bald, and her eyelashes are nearly gone. This isn't due to cancer or age, as many people who know her suspect. She has uncontrollable urges to tug, twist, and pull her hair and lashes. Unless she acts on these urges, the stress increases and becomes overwhelming. Playing with her locks seems to distract her from her anxiety. When Rosa's anxiety magnifies the stress and tension, she impulsively and unconsciously pulls her hair even more. But when she looks in the mirror and sees her balding pate and sparse lashes, she feels ashamed and guilty. She cannot ignore what she has done. As often as she vows to stop, during the three years she has tried, every effort has failed.

Rosa suffers from what is known in technical terms as *trichotillomania*, or TTM. This is an impulse to continually pull at the hair of your scalp, eyelashes, eyebrows, or anywhere else there is hair on your body. Rosa feels a tangible sense of relief when she's touching her hair, but the unease it causes in others and the effect it has on her appearance are humiliating.

Skin picking is an impulse disorder similar to hair pulling except that individuals who suffer from this problem pick their skin—often but not always on the face—to the point of discomfort, loss of function, or disfigurement. As with hair pulling, this act seems to ease a growing inner tension; afterward, it brings on remorse.

Compulsive Shopping and Kleptomania

Barbara has an irresistible urge to buy expensive shoes, jewelry, and handbags, even though she certainly doesn't need any of these items and can't afford them. She can only go a couple of days without making a purchase. After that, she begins to feel so distressed that she practically races to the nearest boutique. She's been known to buy the first pair of shoes she lays her hands on, even if they aren't her size, just to feel a sense of relief. Despite making a decent salary as an executive secretary at an investment bank, Barbara has maxed out her credit cards to the point that she's damaged her credit score and is unable to obtain a mortgage. Sometimes her craving to shop is so strong that she will leave work in the middle of the day; once she even left a friend's baby shower to check out a sale at her favorite department store.

More women than men are compulsive shoppers. Like Barbara, they can't seem to stop buying things they don't need, despite the toll it takes on their finances, relationships, and careers. As with any ICD, shopping allows them to quell their anxiety and gives them a fleeting sense of satisfaction, but after a shopping spree they often feel regret.

Other people feel compelled to steal items they don't need or even value, an affliction known as *kleptomania*. Kleptomaniacs often have the money to pay for what they take, but they steal anyway just for the emotional surge and tension release. What they filch is not for personal gain; it's the act of theft they seem to need. Like most people with impulse control issues, they usually feel remorseful after they've stolen something, yet this doesn't stop their drive to continue.

Pyromania

Gabe's fascination with fire started during his preteens, when he used to help his father burn rubbish in the backyard. Soon he was secretly sneaking out to set fires on his own. Now that he's in his twenties, the urge to light up something is often so overpowering that he feels tense and out of sorts until he acts on the urge. Only the flames seem to calm him down. He knows that starting fires is wrong and dangerous. He doesn't wish to harm anyone, but he feels that he can't help himself.

Pyromania, the compulsion to set fires, is one of the more dangerous types of ICD. There's obvious risk to people and property. It also carries a personal risk as well: if you're caught, there are serious legal consequences. Gabe deliberately sets fires in remote locations to limit his risk. Thank goodness he hasn't done any serious damage yet. He doesn't know why he feels such a strong attraction to fire and fire-starting paraphernalia. He just knows that he feels aroused when watching a blaze. If this describes your relationship with fire, it's possible you might be suffering from pyromania too.

Intermittent Explosive Disorder

When one of Steve's children accidentally spills a drink at the dinner table, the family all hold their breaths waiting to see how he will react. Very often he blows his stack with such forceful rage that they can't continue their meal. It's the same at work: his coworkers never know what will set him off. His outbursts are overblown and seemingly random. Everyone treads lightly when they are around him—or they avoid him altogether. He's so volatile that he recently had a screaming match at the deli when someone took too long to pay for her sandwich. Now he's banned from the store.

Steve doesn't mean to be so explosive. He knows his anger is often out of proportion to the situation, but stress builds up inside him until it suddenly bursts out like a Champagne cork. He usually offers a heartfelt apology for his behavior, but at this point, he's already alienated his colleagues and strained his relationships with his family.

From the description of his behavior, it's likely that Steve is suffering from intermittent explosive disorder (IED). This problem occurs when you are filled with overwhelming rage, even in situations that don't call for such an intense reaction. After your emotional explosion, you feel better for a while—but what about those around you? Despite feeling bad about how you act, you can't take it back. Ultimately, this cycle of rage takes a toll on your personal, professional, and social life. Experts sometimes describe this problem in terms of a specific set of circumstances that trigger the reaction: road rage, air rage, and even soccer mom rage are examples of this disorder.

Newly Recognized Impulse Control Issues

As the world evolves, so do the definitions of ICD. The difficulty controlling urges is sometimes directed in ways that only recently have been recognized. For example, a segment of computer users has difficulty controlling their use of the technology. Some are compelled to compulsively surf the Internet, send e-mail, or chat; others shop, gamble, or watch pornography.

Other patterns of behavior that might have a component of ICD include compulsive gaming, compulsive sexual behavior, and compulsive eating. Whatever the urge, the expression of the disorder typically repeats to deal with the same issue: people with ICD rely on discharging the impulse so that they will feel better. They often recognize that their actions are causing problems, but they have difficulty controlling them anyway.

Is There a Connection Between Your Gambling and Impulse Control?

Think carefully about how any issues you have with impulse control might affect your gambling. Now write down your answers to the following questions in your journal.

1. When do you gamble?
2. How do you usually feel before you gamble? Are you anxious? Nervous? Excited?
3. Now specifically ask yourself, *Do I feel urges to gamble?*
4. If you feel impulses to gamble, do you believe that winning money will limit those urges? How?
5. How do you feel after you've gambled? Relieved? Calmer?
6. Does the strength of your urge to gamble change depending on whether you won or lost money?
7. Do you think it's possible that your impulses are affecting your gambling behavior? If so, how?

MAKING CHANGES

As with any problem in your life, there are three main pathways for addressing your issues with impulse control:

1. Make no attempt to change.
2. Attempt to make changes on your own.
3. Attempt to change with professional help.

You can try to take what works for you from each of these approaches and create your own unique path. You might not yet know which approach you should use when dealing with either impulse control or gambling problems. Perhaps hearing more about the personal stories of Barbara and Steve—two people who took their own journeys toward recovery—will help you decide your best course of action. We'll start with Barbara's journey.

Making No Attempt to Change

Barbara's troubles with ICD began early in life. She'd twirl and twist her hair without realizing she was doing it. She later recalls a sense of emotional release each time she plucked a hair from her head. She struggled with this behavior throughout her teens, but as an adult, she had it largely under control. It had been months since she'd felt the need to play with her hair—that's why what happened shortly after the birth of her first child caught her off guard.

One morning, Barbara woke up feeling anxious and had an overwhelming urge to shop. At first, she didn't think much of it. Gradually the compulsions grew more powerful until she was spending several days a week at the mall or going to some designer sale to buy shoes and accessories she didn't need. Sometimes she'd even wake up late at night with a craving to shop, and she'd surf the Internet and order things online.

Her shopping urges intensified throughout the day until she had the opportunity to spend money. When she finally hit the stores, the relief was so intense it was a kind of high. Because she didn't really need the things she bought, she began to hide her purchases all around the house. Sometimes out of guilt she'd return items. Her shopping was so prolific that the closets, attic, and basement were soon full to bursting with the items she had purchased.

Right around the baby's first birthday, Barbara decided to distract herself from incessant shopping by gambling at a casino located in the next town. Before long, these trips became a daily excursion. Gambling not only provided the same sense of relief as her spending free-for-alls but also helped ease her anxieties about motherhood.

Her husband wasn't pleased that Barbara was gambling, even though she tried to justify it as less destructive than compulsive shopping and hair pulling. She did lose money, but at least gambling didn't leave bald spots or fill up her closets with tangible evidence. Her husband didn't agree with this line of thinking.

For a while, Barbara seemed to replace shopping with gambling. However, for the past several months, every time she's had a winning streak, she stops on the way home to spend the "extra money." Now her husband is beyond angry. He sees their bank account dwindling, and he's accused her of neglecting the baby. During a heated argument, he told her to get herself together or he would leave and take their child with him.

Barbara realizes she has problems, but she's afraid to face up to her fears about motherhood. She's worried she won't be able to stop gambling or shopping even if she tries. She isn't sure she's strong enough to give up the only two activities that dampen her anxiety, give her a rush, and transport her to a more comfortable place—temporary as it is. And even if she gets her shopping and gambling under control, she's not sure her life will be better for it.

Barbara also secretly hopes her problems will clear up on their own. After all, hadn't her hair pulling problem gradually gotten better over time? Maybe the same thing magically will happen in this case. And it's true: sometimes people with impulse control disorders do improve without any help or conscious effort. It's also true that things can get worse before they get better.

So now that you've heard the details of Barbara's story, what do you think? Should she leave things as they are? Or would she be better off taking some steps toward change?

Now ask yourself the same questions about your situation. Are you ready to make changes? If not, why not? What's holding you back? Jot down some thoughts about these questions in your journal. Keep in mind that even if you aren't ready to take steps toward improving your ability to control impulses or lessen your gambling, you might be ready in the future—even the very near future.

Attempting to Make Changes on Your Own

People who make the effort to reduce their symptoms and improve their lives can expect some relief. The type of change that a person makes varies depending on the severity of his or her symptoms; no matter how serious the problems, however, the right combination of tools and support can produce change.

Self-directed change refers to change that you control. A self-help approach requires effort and focus. In the end, self-directed change can be quite effective. It's a good alternative for anyone who wants to change for the better but isn't inclined to seek help from a professional or attend group therapy meetings.

In one sense Barbara is correct: attempting to control impulses and gambling can be a challenge. This will be the case whether you decide to change with or without professional help. Like Barbara, you might genuinely want to take steps to better your life; you also may feel that you don't have the knowledge or energy to begin.

If you stay focused and follow through, you *can* change. The self-help strategies we cover in this section provide you with a lot of valuable information, but *you* must do the work. We don't tell you about the hard work to discourage you from trying or believing that you can succeed. In fact, quite the opposite is true. We simply want you to be prepared for the task ahead so that when you hit the inevitable bumps in the road—as most people do—you will accept them as part of the journey and not use them as a reason to give up. Attempting to change is a success on its own!

Urge Aversion

Part of the reason you act on an impulse is that it helps you release pent-up tension. One way to interrupt or reverse this pattern is with a method known as *aversion therapy*. This is when you associate a rewarding activity—in this case, an impulsive act—with an unpleasant sensation or experience. Afterward, you're less likely to follow through with the impulse; after a while, you are less likely to experience the impulse.

In some countries, cigarette packages include graphic pictures of rotting teeth or damaged lungs as a form of aversion therapy. For example, Canada introduced such warning labels in 2000. Since then, its smoking rates have declined from about 26 percent to about 20 percent, according to Statistics Canada, a Canadian federal government agency. It's unclear how much of this drop is due to labeling, because the country also implemented other tobacco control efforts at the same time. Nevertheless, some experts believe that the warning labels have been effective. Alternatively, it's common for people to snap a rubber band around their wrist whenever they have the urge to snack or to bite their nails. You might consider cleaning the garbage can every time you have the urge to misuse a drug, or sipping a bitter liquid every time you're tempted to buy a scratch ticket.

Now, every time Barbara feels an urge to gamble coming on, she gives a hard snap to a rubber band she wears around her wrist. She is gradually learning to associate the temporary sting of the rubber band with the urge to play casino games. She's selected an aversion tactic that's not dangerous or apt to cause any meaningful injury, just an unpleasant temporary signal.

To build up a resistance to impulsivity, try the following aversive exercise the next time you have an urge to act. You also can practice this exercise by imagining the urge. We'll use Barbara as an example to help you understand this exercise.

During an Urge

- Pick out an unpleasant task you can do easily and conveniently in various situations as a response to a specific urge you wish to change. *Barbara snaps the rubber band against her wrist every time she has the impulse to go to the casino. She wears the band all the time in case the urge strikes when she's not at home.*

- When you notice the urge, say to yourself, "I'm having the urge to . . ." *Every time Barbara feels the urge to gamble, she says to herself, "I'm having an urge to head to the casino so I can gamble."*

- Immediately after you identify the urge, engage in the unpleasant task. *Barbara instantly snaps the band against her wrist.*

- If you decide to act on the urge anyway, engage in the unpleasant task as soon as possible and for the duration of the urge and the behavior. *If Barbara gives in to the urge, she snaps the band against her wrist as she puts her money into a slot or touches her cards.*

Imagining an Urge

- Pick out a safe but an unpleasant task you can do in response to urges that occur in different situations. *Barbara mixes a good dose of cayenne pepper into a glass of warm, salty water and leaves it by her desk.*

- Imagine where you are and what you're doing when you have the urge to gamble. *Barbara's plan is to take a sip every time she has the urge to head for the casino.*

- As you imagine an urge, engage in the unpleasant task. *Whenever the urge to gamble pops into her head, Barbara takes a small sip of the liquid.*

Self-Talk for Managing Impulses and Thoughts

Some people find telling themselves to "stop" a thought or an impulse to be productive; for others, it can produce problems. There is evidence from several large studies that deliberate thought suppression can actually increase the frequency and intensity of the very thoughts one is trying to control. We believe that to avoid this rebound effect, you should express your thoughts first and only then try to manage them. So the goal isn't stopping thoughts—it's getting them under control.

We also believe that as you become more involved with the change process, having the right self-talk in your head can be a very effective tool for managing thoughts, urges, and impulses. With this simple yet powerful exercise, you identify strong and clear phrases and sentences that help you manage urges by talking to yourself. Some examples Barbara uses:

"This urge to gamble will pass with time."

"I am having an urge to go to the casino so I can play the slots and card games. I will wait five minutes, and if the urge is still this intense or more intense, then I'll evaluate whether to act on it."

"Don't get stuck on this impulse to gamble; it will pass, so keep moving forward."

"I have two choices: I can act on this urge or ignore it. If I ignore it, it will pass."

"I am too good a mother to be acting this way."

As you can see, Barbara allows herself to experience the urges, but then takes steps to manage them. Can you think of similar phrases that might help you keep your impulses in check? Write them down in your journal. Make several copies of the phrases and place them in your wallet, on the fridge, on the bathroom mirror, and anywhere you will see them frequently. Similarly, you can surround yourself with positive energy by posting quotes, sayings, or pictures of people who inspire your desire to change. If you have a particular place where you act impulsively (for example, in your room, next to the fridge, in the car), consider placing these little reminders there for a distraction.

Considering the Consequences

When you let urges control your behavior, your actions are likely to have an impact on you and everyone around you. Have you thought about the impact of giving in to your urges? Barbara never gave it much thought until her husband finally reached his breaking point. When he let her know in no uncertain terms what her compulsions had done to their finances, their marriage, and even their child, it woke her up to the gravity of her actions. She finally realized how much damage her behavior was causing.

What about you? Have you truly considered the consequences of your actions for both you and the people you love? Use your journal to write down your responses to the following exercise to help crystallize how surrendering to urges is affecting your life.

- Imagine one of the urges you commonly struggle with controlling.
- Imagine giving in to that urge.
- What are the possible personal consequences of acting on this urge?
- Who else might be affected? How will they be affected?
- What do you stand to gain in the short term and in the long term by giving in to this urge?
- What do you stand to lose in the short term and in the long term by giving in to this urge?
- Do the gains outweigh the losses?

Self-Monitoring

It's not easy to notice when an urge is coming on. By the time you realize how you feel, you might find yourself already engaged in an impulsive act. The key to changing your behavior is to adjust the thought patterns that lead to the behavior. Once you assess your typical thoughts and reactions, you'll have a basis for change.

Barbara experiences a whirlwind of thoughts, emotions, and concerns before she shops impulsively or gambles. She's uptight about motherhood, upset that she isn't handling things better, overwhelmed with responsibility, and worried that she's not up to the task. There is so much swirling in her head that it's difficult to tease out exactly what leads her down the path toward impulsivity.

Like Barbara, many people with ICDs have difficulty distinguishing their urge triggers. With practice, it's possible to raise your awareness of what heightens your urges so that you can learn to regulate them. It's important to think about which moods seem to lead to more urges. It also is important to learn about what mood you are in once your urge has passed. Also, are there particular thoughts that seem to "green-light" an urge? Do you have periods of time when urges are more frequent and intense? Can you pinpoint when this happens? Are there any thoughts, feelings, or strategies that seem to help you resist or manage urges—even if this is only sometimes?

By tuning in to triggers from the past while becoming more aware of your vulnerability to specific kinds of urges, you'll develop the ability to manage them proactively. Once you're able to recognize your urges, the next step is to monitor their frequency and intensity. Eventually, you will start to notice some patterns. After you've collected enough personal data in your journal, you can make some generalizations about your triggers and urges.

Managing Your Impulses

Every time you do something impulsive, record your information on this form. (You might consider copying it into your journal.) Although it's best to get the information down as you are experiencing the growing tension that leads toward impulsive behavior, you might not always be in a position to do so. Do the best you can to write down your thoughts as close as possible to the actual events. Gradually, this exercise will teach you to recognize what drives your impulses and urges.

In the first row of the chart, record the impulses you feel. In rows 2 and 3, record where you are and what you are doing when you first notice that urge. In rows 4 and 5, record the thoughts and feelings associated with the urge. In row 6, write down whether you acted on the urge. In row 7, record the intensity of the urge, using a scale of 0 to 10, where 0 is not at all intense and 10 is as intense as you have ever experienced. Then, in row 8, note how long the urge lasted before it subsided. If you didn't act, describe in row 9 what kept you from doing so; if you did act, skip to row 10 and describe what you could have done instead. In the final row, rate how hard the urge was to manage using a 0 to 10 scale, where 0 is very easy and 10 is very difficult.

1	Impulsive behavior			
2	Where			
3	What			
4	Thoughts			
5	Feelings			
6	Actions			
7	Intensity of urge			
8	Duration of urge			
9	If no act, why not?			
10	If an act, what are the alternatives?			
11	Effort to manage urge			

Sometimes it's difficult to find the words to describe emotional states and feelings. To help you describe the moods or feelings that might precipitate your impulse, refer to the checklist. It includes a wide range of moods, thoughts, and feelings that commonly trigger impulses.

- ☐ Anxious
- ☐ Manic
- ☐ Irritated
- ☐ Ashamed
- ☐ Helpless
- ☐ Embarrassed
- ☐ Pathetic
- ☐ Rejected
- ☐ Energetic
- ☐ Abandoned
- ☐ Panicked
- ☐ Bored
- ☐ Loving
- ☐ Optimistic
- ☐ Overjoyed

- ☐ Insecure
- ☐ Frustrated
- ☐ Annoyed
- ☐ Guilty
- ☐ Indecisive
- ☐ Tense
- ☐ Lonely
- ☐ Restless
- ☐ Content
- ☐ Agitated
- ☐ Dull
- ☐ Empty
- ☐ Curious
- ☐ Confident
- ☐ Thinking about using substances

- ☐ Depressed
- ☐ Angry
- ☐ Resentful
- ☐ Hopeless
- ☐ Abused
- ☐ Vulnerable
- ☐ Grieving
- ☐ Disadvantaged
- ☐ Relaxed
- ☐ Mistreated
- ☐ Cynical
- ☐ Critical
- ☐ Daring
- ☐ Rebellious
- ☐ Thinking about gambling

Controlling Urges with Relaxation

Being relaxed helps you feel calm, level headed, and able to deal with your thoughts, feelings, and actions. When you're feeling tense or nervous, you're more likely to give in to impulses and behave in ways that you might later regret. Tension, anxiety, and nervousness cannot coexist with relaxation. By its very definition, relaxation reduces tension and arousal. When you are more relaxed, you might experience urges less frequently and find them easier to manage.

It's important to practice getting into a relaxed state even when you aren't feeling impulsive. That way, when you do feel urges bubbling up to the surface, you'll have the necessary skills and experience to help manage your emotions and behavior more effectively. We've outlined several effective relaxation exercises in Chapters Five and Eight. Many of these exercises use the relationship between your mind and body to calm your thoughts and relax your muscles. These tools will help take you out of an agitated state so that you can refocus and be more successful in managing your urges. Be sure to review these exercises. Try them all and decide which ones work best for you to change your impulsive urges.

Managing Specific Impulses

Although many of the tools we've described in this chapter work for all types of ICDs, there are some tools that are applicable to a specific type. If you feel that you are suffering from one type of ICD, these tools might prove especially useful to you.

Hair Pulling

Hair pullers aren't always aware of their impulses at the time they're experiencing them. Barbara, for example, often played with her hair while she was reading or talking on the phone. It can be effective to raise awareness about hair pulling while you are in the act. The following strategies might help.

- Place adhesive bandages on your fingertips or wear gloves so that when you touch your hair, it feels a little strange and makes your hair more difficult to grasp.

- Spray cologne or perfume on your wrists and hands so that when you touch your hair, you'll notice the smell.
- Wear a hat or get a shorter hairstyle so that pulling your hair is more difficult or at least different.
- Clip your fingernails so that gripping or pulling hair is more of a challenge.
- Engage in an incompatible default activity so that your hands aren't free for hair pulling. You might squeeze a ball, roll some Silly Putty around in your hands, or knit during the times and situations you tend to play with your hair.
- Replace the sensation you feel when your hair is being pulled out with another feeling. Some people play with their hair because of the pressures and sensations they feel while doing it. Replacing this sensation can quell the urge. For example, you might try touching a nylon stocking or some other soft material you find appealing to touch. If you like touching facial hair, you might get regular facials or, if you tend to bite your hair, try chewing gum so that you keep your mouth occupied for an extended period of time.
- Avoid triggers. Try to anticipate triggering situations so that you can prepare to manage or avoid them altogether. Common triggers for people who pull hair are mirrors, tweezers, being alone and unobserved, and boredom. Doing the awareness exercises we described earlier can help you get a handle on your triggers.

Kleptomania

The following strategies can help reduce the urge to steal things you don't need or want.

- Kleptomaniacs often benefit from changing or avoiding situations that lead to their urges to steal. Do you have a certain bag or equipment you use to hide or transport your pilfered items? Leave these things at home or toss them out altogether.
- If you believe you'd be less likely to steal things if you were with someone else, try arranging for a friend to go into stores with you as much as possible. Seek companionship especially at times when you most often feel your urges bubble up.

- Consider the consequences. As we mentioned earlier in this chapter, it sometimes helps to consider the consequences of your impulsive acts. In the case of kleptomania, it might help to get out your journal and write a hypothetical story about getting caught stealing. Focus your story on the consequences of your actions and consider the worst-case scenario, the reactions of other people, and the thoughts and feelings you have when you are caught in the act. This exercise is most effective when you do it while you have no urge to steal. Write out several scenarios. When the urge does strike, read what you've written so that you get a taste of what will happen if you follow through on your impulses.

Shopping

The following strategies can be useful for getting compulsive shopping under control.

- When you have an urge to shop, take your money and credit cards from your wallet. Even though going to the mall without the means to buy something can seem unbearable, the urge to shop will pass. Remember, urges always pass. Some people find that window shopping is enough to subvert their urges. Be careful, though; sometimes window shopping is a trigger to buy. You also can try shopping with a friend if you tend to slow down your buying when you're with others. However, choose your friends wisely; some people will encourage you to spend more than you intend.

- People with shopping urges also can benefit from some self-regulation in the form of goals. We cover goal setting extensively in Chapter Two; go back and review the detailed, step-by-step process of assigning an effective goal; then you can apply these principles specifically to shopping impulses. For instance, you might set an explicit budget and walk into the stores with a precise dollar amount you can spend. Then, get out a calculator and track everything that goes into your basket to the penny, including sales tax. You might shop from a list, with the objective to buy only things that appear on the list.

- You might consider some self-help financial counseling services for people who have difficulty controlling their impulses to shop. There are free online services available and sites that monitor how much you spend by price range and category. Some even send you an alert when you exceed your budget.

- Deciding what to spend is part of an internal monologue. Excessive shoppers often tell themselves something that makes it acceptable to buy things. They might think or even say things like "It's on sale," "I deserve this," and "Everyone I know has one of these. I need it too." Transform this internal talk from a monologue to a dialogue. Create reverse statements to use when you find yourself justifying purchases. For example, when you think, "I need this," you can turn this around to "The only things I need are my health and my family." There are many responses to justification statements; find the ones that work best for you. The exercise in Turning Monologues into Dialogues can help you do just that.

Turning Monologues into Dialogues

In your journal, write down the typical internal monologue statements that you use to justify shopping. Next, create an alternative dialogue response statement. Review this exercise on a daily basis so that you are very familiar with your dialogue responses and they readily come to mind whenever the urge to shop strikes. We've listed monologue statements that are common among compulsive shoppers. Add your own personal dialogue rebuttals.

Monologue Statement	Dialogue Response
"It's on sale."	_____
"I deserve this."	_____
"I need this."	_____
"I work hard and earn enough."	_____
"Everyone else has this; I should have it too."	_____
"I will feel better if I buy this."	_____

Skin Picking

People who have the impulse to pick their skin find it challenging to stop. Many do so mindlessly. Some pick only when they go to the bathroom, so it becomes part of their routine. It's possible to stop skin picking. There's a chance that one of the following strategies can work for you:

- If you pick your skin in the bathroom or another specific room, try setting a kitchen timer for three to five minutes, just enough time to use the room but perhaps not enough time to start picking. Once the timer goes off, leave the room.
- As with hair pulling, changing a sensation can be helpful. Putting bandages on your fingers, wearing gloves, or spraying your hands with perfume can be sensory cues not to pick. Keeping your hands occupied with other things can also be a successful substitution strategy.
- Skin picking on the face is commonly triggered by looking in the mirror. Try spraying your mirror with just enough white craft spray (sometimes called fake snow) that you can still see through to shave or put on makeup. The spray isn't permanent, so you can take it off when you're ready to use the mirror in a usual way. Alternatively, you can dim or color the lights around your mirror so that you won't notice blemishes as much.
- Sometimes people who pick at their skin have an elaborate skin care routine that can exacerbate their skin issues and heighten the impulse to pick. Consult with a dermatologist and discuss your trouble with regulating skin picking. Dermatologists often have considerable experience with this issue and can provide a personalized treatment program.

Intermittent Explosive Disorder

Many of the general strategies we covered earlier in this section can be useful for dealing with explosive emotional outbursts. The advice about learning to relax can be particularly pertinent. The exercises located here and in Chapters Five and Eight can help you identify the signs of growing tension and anger and head them off before they escalate into a burst of anger that you'll regret later. The following are some specific strategies you might try.

- As you have learned, changing your internal monologue can help you see things differently and prevent an overwhelming reaction. Ask yourself, *Will any of this matter a year from now?* Quite often the answer is no. You also might say to yourself things like "Frustration, irritation, annoyance, and unfairness are a part of life" or "Getting angry about the problem is not a solution" or "This problem might be making me really mad, but exploding over it is a much bigger problem." Write these in your journal and consider carrying a list of statements around with you so that you can look at them often and reduce your number of outbursts.

- Express yourself. When you act angrily, you might think that you are expressing yourself—after all, you are acting consistently with the way you feel. However, this connection between feelings and behavior is not working for you. You do have alternatives. You can learn to communicate with measured language and ideas rather than with aggression and physical violence. When you are calm, think about your feelings and share them with others. Discharging your feelings in small pieces through conversation will minimize the tension and anger. Also stay logical so that you can express yourself effectively. If communicating to someone about your feelings is too difficult, write the conversation on paper first to become comfortable with the ideas.

TIPS FOR USEFUL COMMUNICATION

- State your feelings in detail.
- Stay specific. Name the problems that led to your anger, even if you created some of these difficulties yourself.
- Avoid broad, blanket statements like "You always . . ." or "You never . . ."
- Resist jumping to conclusions; recognize when you do.
- Avoid insulting, blaming, or putting others down.
- Try listening to what others have to say.
- Have a plan in case you begin to feel an urge to retaliate. Retaliation is more explosiveness and will not solve the underlying issues.
- When all else fails, walk away. This will give you an opportunity to take a few deep breaths and think about alternatives.
- Learn to accept that frustrating, inconvenient, and annoying things happen. You might think that things "ought" to go your way, but "ought" is not reality. Accepting what happens in the here and now is your best strategy for staying calm.

Attempting to Change with Professional Help

As you may recall, you met Steve earlier in this chapter. He was given to emotional, angry outbursts that were usually a vast overreaction to the circumstances. To those around him, these outbursts seemed to come out of nowhere. Coworkers, friends, and family never knew what would set him off. Everyone, including his wife and children, had begun to feel genuinely afraid of him. They'd tiptoe around him, trying their best not to set him off.

One of the few things that temporarily calmed Steve down was playing Internet poker. He would lose himself in the activity and play for hours. When he was winning or at least breaking even, playing online poker worked to keep him from exploding. However, a losing streak would often be the thing to ignite a tantrum. His wife was concerned about his gambling, but she was too afraid to speak to him about it because she feared it would set him off. Steve regretted his behavior but couldn't seem to help himself. Try as he might to control it, he frequently felt the tension building up inside of him until it boiled over into a rage-filled tirade. One day at work, he was playing poker on his computer and lost a big bet. It set him off big-time, and he threatened to hit a secretary who made a mistake putting his presentation together. He didn't follow through with the threat, but it scared the secretary enough that she reported him to human resources. HR told him that he must seek counseling for both his rage and his gambling or he'll be terminated. Feeling he had no choice, Steve agreed.

Counseling is a good step for Steve and others who have tried and failed many times to manage their wrath-filled impulses and believe their gambling might be tied to their out-of-control behavior. Anyone who finds it overwhelming to control impulses on his own—and who truly wants to change—should consider seeking professional help. For some people, this is the best strategy for controlling their gambling-related and other impulses.

Steve began seeing a psychologist, who has diagnosed him with intermittent explosive disorder (IED). He's also enrolled himself in an anger management program that includes a weekly group meeting. Steve has seen his physician to explore any possible physiological issues. So far, his tests have come back normal, though his doctor has explained that his issues could be the result of an imbalance of brain chemicals. Steve and his doctor are weighing the potential benefits of medication as they evaluate the effects of the other treatments.

Steve seems to be benefiting from therapy and group meetings. What he learns in sessions and meetings has challenged his negative views of the world and of other people. This new worldview seems to help reduce the intensity and frequency of his violent episodes and,

Although some people find that their urges are less intense when they use certain medications, medication does not work for everyone. Researchers have found better results by combining medication with behavior therapy.

as a result, his gambling is now under control. He's been reframing his idea of "manliness" in terms of self-control rather than as something to be "proved" through aggression and anger.

Although Steve is doing well in therapy and even beginning to successfully employ some of the self-help strategies we've discussed in this chapter, he and his doctor think it's a good idea for him to take medication. Several medications have been used for treating IED. These include carbamazepine (Tegretol), an antiseizure medication; propranolol (Inderal), a heart medication that controls blood pressure and irregular heart rhythms; and lithium, a drug used to stabilize moods.

With medication, therapy, and self-help techniques, Steve is turning his life around. A year into his treatment, he's learned that stress is a trigger for his outbursts. He works hard at maintaining calm and resisting the impulse to blow his stack at every little perceived infraction. He has completely curtailed his online poker. As a result, his relationship with his kids and his wife has improved immensely, and he's having a much easier time at work.

Psychological disorders such as IED and other ICDs develop for a number of reasons. There is, for instance, some evidence to suggest that certain chemical imbalances in the brain might influence ICD and that hormones, such as testosterone, can act as contributors. Other factors, such as stress, genetics, and environment, play a role. You might find that you can't get to the root of your problems on your own. If this is the case, getting help from a trained, experienced professional, as Steve ultimately did, can be invaluable.

Far from being a copout, seeking help is a very brave thing to do. You admit to yourself that you have a problem and that you aren't succeeding in dealing with it on your own, and, therefore, you seek professional help to try to make things better. You aren't ceding your responsibility; you are taking control. You'll still need to put in a significant amount of time and effort. When you succeed, the payoff will be worth it.

If you've tried to deal with your ICD and gambling on your own but haven't succeeded, perhaps it's time for you to consider getting some help. Treatment providers will work with you to address impulsive behaviors and the consequences of those behaviors. Social workers, psychologists, and psychiatrists all have professional training that focuses on impulse management. These professionals have the skills and knowledge to help you find the right therapist to design a treatment program that targets your impulse control and gambling-related problems.

You and a professional can create a plan—one that will be manageable, reasonable, revisable, and based on your strengths, weaknesses, problems, and the changes you make—to help work through your problems. Treatment plans can include working through related mental health problems, such as anxiety and depression. Your past efforts won't be without value because you can show your treatment professionals your previous work and your journal to help them gain a better understanding of the challenges you've faced and the strategies you've attempted.

You needn't be embarrassed about seeking outside help. Although you are free to tell loved ones about your recovery efforts, you don't have to advertise the fact that you're working with a mental health professional. It's a private matter. You don't have to tell anyone, and the professional is not ethically allowed to reveal any of the details of your therapy. If you decide to attend group meetings, members are obliged to honor a privacy oath.

Getting help doesn't mean losing the support of your loved ones, either; it just means getting a different kind of help. Friends and family might try to understand your issues; however, quite often they lack the expertise and skills to provide the degree or type of assistance you require. Mental health clinicians spend many years learning about emotional problems, suffering, and how to change behavior patterns. They possess the skills and resources to help you; usually these skills are more advanced than those of your friends and family. Remember, sometimes discussing your problems with a stranger—someone who doesn't have a stake in your personal life— can give you fresh insight.

WHERE DO YOU GO FROM HERE?

We hope that, after reading this chapter, you have chosen a pathway to changing your relationship with ICD and gambling. Just reading this chapter is an important first step toward recovery. However, maybe you're not ready to make any real changes right now. If that's the case, this is not a cause for concern. You don't have to feel rushed into making a decision. This book is full of information, tools, and resources that you can use to help make your decision—whenever you are ready. If you are not ready for change now, this doesn't mean you will never be interested in making changes. After all, we are always changing whether we like it or not. Most likely, you will be ready for change later.

If you do decide to implement some of the self-help tools we've described or to work with professional help as you deal with ICD and gambling, be ready: you might slip up and relapse to previous patterns. Relapse is part of recovery. Don't become discouraged. Instead, try to pick up where you left off, but make sure you examine what led to the lapse or relapse. Review your experiences, thoughts, and feelings before, during, and after your impulses. In your journal, keep a log of your efforts; this will help identify your impulse triggers so that you can work with them. Congratulate yourself for taking steps toward recovery; know that any effort is an accomplishment. We're confident that with lots of work and effort, you can make desirable changes to your impulses and your gambling behavior.

8

Substance Abuse and Gambling

What you'll learn in this chapter: If you're concerned about how much you drink or use other drugs, or if you think your substance use has an effect on your gambling, then the information in this chapter is important. We describe the signs and symptoms of substance use disorder, discuss how these relate to and influence gambling, and suggest different ways of improving your life, with a particular emphasis on self-help strategies.

There's a common misperception in our society that people with alcohol or other drug addiction are simply being socially irresponsible and morally weak. The feeling is that they can stop their behavior at any time if they really wanted to and if only they put their mind to it. This view underestimates the complexity of addiction. Psychoactive drugs, such as alcohol, alter the function of the brain and sometimes change its structure as well. For some people, this means that drinking and drug use lead to abuse and dependence. For them, it isn't just a matter of willpower or judgment; they have physical, biochemical urges that can be difficult to change.

It's also true that the initial decision to start drinking or taking other drugs is a personal choice. Some people can have a few drinks after work or a cocktail on the weekend with no ill effects, and some

155

people can take other drugs—legal or otherwise—without too many negative consequences. But for some people, repeated drug use changes the brain and affects their self-control and their ability to make good decisions; these changes magnify their impulses to keep drinking or drugging.

Unfortunately, there isn't any easy screening or a single factor that can predict who will become addicted and who won't. There's evidence that some people do have a genetic predisposition toward addiction. Sometimes a traumatic event such as a brain injury can be the catalyst for the start of the behavior. Environmental and social factors as well as peer pressure and stress also can play a role in determining drug use and abuse. None of this means that someone with substance abuse issues can't turn his or her life around. Research also backs up the idea that there are many different successful strategies and treatments for recovery.

Once you make the decision to stop drinking or taking other drugs, you have some work ahead of you. There's no way to sugarcoat this fact. You might not accomplish your goals immediately, and that might be frustrating. You might even feel like giving up sometimes. However, just admitting the need to make a change in your life and admitting that you're scared, but willing to try, is a critical step toward improving your life. You move closer and closer to recovery simply by *trying*.

Think of the other side of things too: over time, through hard work, you will learn new skills, either from this book or from other resources, and integrate these into your daily life. These skills will help you improve your relationship with alcohol and other drugs—and with gambling too. These skills also might help you feel significantly better about yourself, your relationships, and many other aspects of your life.

So let's start by understanding what substance abuse and substance dependence are all about. You'll meet some people in this chapter who have struggled with both substance use and gambling. We hope that their stories will help you understand your own struggles. We'll also present plenty of strategies—especially those focused on taking a self-help approach—that can help you gain control of your addiction and your life.

SUBSTANCE ABUSE

Xavier had a motto when he was younger: work hard; play hard. After a long day as an exec at a prestigious marketing firm, he liked to hit the bars with his buddies and gamble a bit. As he was moving his way up the ranks at work, he met his wife while out clubbing one weekend, and within a few months they were married with a baby on the way. He hadn't planned for everything to move so quickly, but he tried to roll with it. He cut back on the partying and came home every night to his new family. For a while he was happy.

MANAGING DRUG WITHDRAWAL

When alcohol or other drugs alter your state of mind and your normal capacity to act in a reasonable manner, you're experiencing *substance intoxication*. This effect varies from person to person, and it certainly varies with personal tolerance, amount of drug use, and type of substance. When someone cuts back or eliminates the use of a specific substance, they often go through the *substance withdrawal* symptoms associated with that type of substance dependence. For opioids, these symptoms can include a racing pulse, feelings of hot or cold, vomiting, and diarrhea. Alcohol and sedative withdrawal symptoms can be severe; for example, the DTs, or delirium tremens, can include hallucinations and seizures. Because the withdrawal effects of alcohol and sedatives can be life threatening, if you've used them in sufficient amounts and for prolonged periods, don't go it alone. Contact a medical professional before reducing or eliminating your use. Withdrawal from these drugs can be very dangerous.

> You can have a substance abuse problem yet still hold down a job. But proper treatment can help you start on a career path, rise in your career, and feel better while working and navigating through life. Getting your substance use under control can definitely help you ease many of your burdens.

As time passed and Xavier's responsibilities grew, he felt the pressure mount. To blow off some steam, he started purchasing an occasional scratch ticket at the bodega around the corner from his office. One day, he won $500 on a $2 ticket. That seemed to flip a switch in his head: all of a sudden his gambling—and then his drinking—turned into something else.

Now he couldn't go an afternoon without missing his ticket or his gin and tonic. He started playing poker for high stakes wherever he could find a game. Instead of going to his kid's school plays or gymnastics meets, he started hanging out at the local bar and anywhere else he could to play cards and bet. His work performance began to slip; it was only because he was so experienced that he was able to hold it together.

One night while driving home after too many cocktails, he side-swiped another car and almost ran it off the road. Thankfully no one was seriously injured. But now Xavier's saddled with a mountain of legal trouble and a DUI on his record. His drinking and gambling already were a source of friction between Xavier and his wife. This latest incident sent their relationship over the edge. She's demanding he clean up his act; he's insisting that everything is under control.

Even if he isn't ready to admit it, Xavier is having issues with *substance abuse* and gambling addiction. If your drinking or use of substances (legal or otherwise) causes you to shirk your obligations or affects your performance at work or your other relationships, or if you find yourself in physically hazardous situations (for example, engaging in impaired driving) because of your drinking or substance use, or if your drinking or substance use has resulted in legal problems, then you too may be dealing with a form of substance abuse.

SUBSTANCE DEPENDENCE

Rebecca's doctor first prescribed OxyContin for her to help her deal with the pain from injuries she suffered after a bad car accident. It took her nearly a year to get back on her feet. During that time, she was restricted and couldn't get around very well. She took the pain-killer every day, gradually escalating the dose so that she could still feel a buzz. When she began refilling her prescriptions at a faster pace than expected, her doctor scolded her and told her to slow down; she smiled and said she would—then made an appointment with a different doctor for a second prescription and filled it at a different pharmacy in another neighborhood. Rebecca began to feel depressed about her circumstances.

When it finally came time to wean herself off the drug, she was surprised by how hard it was. Every time she tried to stop or cut back, she felt as though she was coming down with a severe case of the flu; her muscles would ache right down to her bones, and she couldn't stop the diarrhea and vomiting. Finally she'd relent and take another pill. In fact, she'd dissolve it in water and gulp it down to speed up the effects of the drug and increase the rush. Pretty soon she was seeing several doctors and inventing elaborate stories so that she could get more and more prescriptions. During this time, her depression worsened, and she started to gamble at the new casino in her town. She could sit at a casino without having to move, so it was easy both to avoid the pain and to distract herself from it. She noticed that she felt less depressed when she was gambling.

Rebecca now realizes she has a serious drug problem, but she doesn't know what to do about it. She's never had any issue with drugs before and doesn't consider herself "the type" to ever become addicted. But is she addicted?

In clinical terms, we would say that Rebecca is *substance dependent*. This circumstance is characterized by a marked need for the substance of choice as well as a need to take increasing amounts of the substance to get the same "high" and to avoid withdrawal symptoms. People struggling with substance dependence often take more of their "drug of choice" (which could be alcohol) than they intend, even though they might wish to cut back or stop. Often, they spend a good deal of time, effort, and energy trying to obtain the substance and trying to recover from its effects after they use it. They also might find themselves curtailing social and work obligations to persist in their usage even after they realize their problems are becoming worse.

GAMBLING AND SUBSTANCE ABUSE

People like Rebecca and Xavier who struggle with both gambling issues and substance abuse are by no means rare. Research shows that whereas 13 percent of the population suffers from alcohol abuse or dependence at some point in their life, among pathological gamblers, the numbers skyrocket: more than 25 percent are dealing with alcohol abuse, and nearly 50 percent are considered alcohol dependent. About 9 percent of the general population suffers from some form of substance abuse or dependence other than alcohol and tobacco; in addition, approximately 38 percent of pathological gamblers abuse or are dependent on illegal drugs.

For some gamblers, gambling helps them escape the problems caused by their substance use. For others, gambling provides the opportunity to release tension. In either of these cases, gambling stimulates emotional experiences that allow people to separate from their daily life. Under some conditions, gamblers experience a temporary escape from problems without having to deal with them. Others start gambling before their substance use or life problems get too out of control; in this case, it's the gambling that ultimately leads to the unintended negative consequences that affect their health, relationships, and financial well-being. For this group, the adverse

Is There a Connection Between Your Gambling and Your Substance Use?

Ask yourself how your drinking or substance use is related to your gambling. Think carefully about this and write down your answers to the following questions.

1. Which came first, your issues with gambling or your issues with drinking and other substance abuse?
2. How do you think the two issues are related?
3. Do you tend to drink or abuse drugs in larger amounts when you gamble?
4. Do you gamble more recklessly when you have been drinking or abusing drugs?
5. Do you gamble more often when you are under the influence?
6. Do drinking or substance abuse and gambling always or nearly always go hand in hand? Or are there times when you do one without the other?

consequences of gambling precipitate their substance abuse. In Xavier's case, for example, his daily trip to the bodega for a scratch ticket and the few hours he spends playing cards are his ways of forgetting about his responsibilities; when he started adding a few gin and tonics to the experience, it was simply his way of extending the experience of the escape.

MAKING CHANGES

There are three main options or pathways to help you face your issues with drinking too much and substance abuse:

1. Make no attempt to change.
2. Attempt to make changes on your own.
3. Attempt to change with professional help.

We'll carefully outline each of these pathways for you, but they aren't mutually exclusive. Feel free to take what you need from each; you also can learn from and use sources other than this book. Recovery and change is a personal journey. Although we can offer you supportive information and resources, ultimately you must take charge and decide what works best for you.

Making No Attempt to Change

You can decide to do nothing about your drinking or drug problems or about how much you gamble. That is certainly the path of least resistance. It also might be the path of least reward. Both our clinical work and research show that it's possible for your behavior and your life to improve on their own, even if you make no effort whatsoever— but it's also possible that your problems will get worse with time.

You need to think long and hard about what you are getting out of leaving things as they are. Rebecca doesn't feel ready to face the hard work it would take to make changes. She sees some advantages in not taking any steps toward improving her life. She won't have to go through the difficult process of trying to get better. Where she is right now is at least familiar; after getting a taste of withdrawal symptoms, she fears that recovery could be far worse than the addiction itself.

However, once she is willing to turn her thoughts around and look at some of the negatives of staying dependent on OxyContin, she might decide that these outweigh the positives. She's probably damaging some important relationships in her life as well as shirking some personal and professional responsibilities. She also expends a lot of time, effort, and energy juggling all the stories, different doctors, and different pharmacies. Her use has begun holding her back in many areas of her life, and she knows that down the road it might even lead to some very serious legal and personal problems.

Like Rebecca, you need to ask yourself: *Do the pros really outweigh the cons here? Do I really think doing nothing about my substance use and gambling is the right way to go? Don't I owe it to myself to at least try to make improvements in my life?*

Attempting to Make Changes on Your Own

Xavier has always prided himself on keeping his gambling and drinking private, but one day he became acutely aware that he hadn't done as good a job of hiding his patterns as he had imagined. After returning from the bar one afternoon not long after his car accident, he overheard one of his employees describe him as being exactly like someone he grew up with. "He's just like my Uncle Ronnie—there's always a slight smell of alcohol on him. And his mood seems to depend on how strong the smell is on any given day."

This was yet another wakeup call for Xavier. Combined with his troubles from the accident, both at work and on the home front, this moment made it abundantly clear how much his drinking and gambling are causing his life to unravel. At last he feels it's time to try to make a change. He doesn't feel comfortable going to a therapist or group meetings, but he does think he is now ready to try to pull his life together on his own.

One thing that has been holding Xavier back is the fear that trying to control his substance use will make his problems with gambling worse, or vice versa. In any event, it's likely that he'll experience urges to gamble or use alcohol for the rest of his life. In time he will learn to master these urges. Unless he tries to do so, he will never know that he can.

Xavier also worries about how changing his relationship with drinking and gambling will transform his personal relationships. Now these activities are the center of his social life. He leans on his drinking and gambling buddies for support and understanding. He realizes that if he cuts back or stops drinking or gambling completely, he might not see his friends as often. At the same time, he realizes that some of these friendships are based purely on risky behaviors. Consequently, as painful as it is to do so, Xavier might be better off

Symptoms of withdrawal can range from mildly uncomfortable to seriously dangerous. Alcohol withdrawal can have a particularly negative effect on your health. If you are planning on reducing or eliminating heavy, chronic drug or alcohol use, we strongly recommend speaking to a medical professional about how to do so safely.

moving on from them. And he knows that this is an opportunity to change his relationships with friends and family who aren't involved with his substance use or gambling. These relationships have crumbled under the weight of his addiction, and this is his chance to try to heal them.

The type of doubts that Xavier has shouldn't keep you from trying to recover. Gaining control of substance use and gambling on your own requires a great deal of effort and discipline; it's also a process that can lead to substantial rewards. If you think you're experiencing adverse consequences from substance use, gambling, or a combination of the two and you'd like things in your life to get better, you're probably ready to make changes. However, if you don't think that right now is the best time to seek additional help from others, such as treatment from a professional, self-help might be the most appropriate approach for you. You should know that by choosing the self-directed path, you have a lot of hard work ahead of you, and some of that work might be physically uncomfortable or downright unpleasant. If you succeed, the payoff will be well worth it.

Moderation Versus Abstinence

When thinking about recovery from substance abuse, you're really faced with two choices: you can try to moderate your use of alcohol and other substances, or you can abstain completely. Actually, the same is true for any type of addiction, including gambling.

If you choose to simply moderate your behavior, your list of options grows. In Xavier's case, he could choose to cut back his drinking to the weekends or decide that he will have gin and tonics only when life gets a little too hectic. He might limit just his drinking, or he could decide to limit both his drinking and his gambling. Really, any combination of moderate drinking and gambling is possible; however, Xavier must view the change as an improvement—that is, moderation must, in fact, make a difference in how well Xavier is able to function.

Moderation of any sort might demonstrate to Xavier's family and colleagues that he's capable of controlling his behavior. It might be enough to regain their trust and respect—but it might not. In particular, his wife might not see the act of cutting back as enough progress for her to feel happy about it. For that matter, the court might not view it favorably when his drunken driving case comes up for review. So even though in Xavier's mind he's made a good-faith effort, others in his life might not see it that way. The result is that moderation might not have as much of a positive effect on his life as Xavier wishes.

Another reason moderation might not be the best path for Xavier and many other substance abusers is that there's little proof that it will work out in the long term. It could be that using even a little of the substance is enough to keep your urges alive; also, using intoxicating substances can impair judgment so that it's difficult to make good choices. The evidence is complicated for people who attempt moderation. Some research shows that about half of the people who resolved their alcohol problems for at least one year returned later to moderate drinking. Usually, these were people who experienced less severe drinking problems. Among those in their first year of recovery who tried to abstain completely from alcohol and other drugs, only 10 to 15 percent didn't lapse; lapsing is different from moderate drug use after recovery. Therefore, the majority of people who struggle with any kind of substance use problem must be prepared to manage lapses and relapses. (See Chapter Nine for information about relapse prevention.) Complicating all of this, experts cannot predict who is likely to lapse or relapse.

Now, what if Xavier chooses complete abstinence? What would this mean, and what would it entail? Ending both his substance abuse and gambling would give him the greatest hope of keeping his job, his family, and his health; and it might help mitigate the consequences of his legal situation. It also might mean that he'd have to endure a difficult change process and possibly even some physical symptoms of withdrawal. Xavier's long-term goal in choosing abstinence would be to stop all of his problematic behaviors—buying scratch tickets, participating in card games, and drinking—completely.

Until this point, Xavier's addiction has played a significant role in his life. To give up gambling and drinking entirely, even for a short amount of time, has been nearly unthinkable in the past because he knows that abstinence, like moderation, can end in relapse. He hasn't been able to imagine suffering through "cold turkey" only to slide back into his old ways. It's a proposition he was not ready to face until now. He needs to understand that no matter what path he takes to recovery, there's always a chance he'll relapse. The chance is higher with moderation than with abstinence. And no matter what, he will need to have a plan in place in case of relapse. Every person recovering from addiction must be prepared and ready for this possibility, regardless of which pathway to recovery he or she chooses.

When choosing between moderation and abstinence, you will find it useful to know that many recovering people think that abstinence is easier to accomplish than moderation. Perhaps it's an out of sight, out of mind mentality. For some, cutting back feels closer to their current situation than choosing to abstain entirely; their problem activities remain front and center and still require constant effort to control. Also, moderation might yield only moderate and slow improvement, whereas abstinence, though initially more challenging, is likely to yield greater rewards more quickly. With all this in mind, let's work through some questions to help you decide whether moderation or abstinence is the best course of action for you right now.

1. What will you gain by continuing to engage in substance use and gambling, even if you cut back from where you are right now?
2. Would you gain more if you stopped entirely?
3. There is a possibility that you will not be successful at moderating your behavior the first time you try. Are you willing to risk being unsuccessful in your attempt to modify your addictive behaviors?
4. Is there a possibility that you can't abstain entirely from substance use and gambling at this time? Are you willing to take this risk?
5. Long term, what do you predict will be the results of choosing to moderate versus abstain from your substance use or gambling?
6. Do you want only a modest change to your current lifestyle, or do you want much larger changes?
7. Putting aside the question of moderation versus abstinence for the moment, do you have a plan of action if you should relapse? What is it?

After giving it a lot of thought and asking himself these same tough questions, Xavier has chosen the path of total abstinence from drinking and gambling. Originally, he wanted to drink and gamble in moderation. However, he's decided that he wants his family back and wants to keep his job. He doesn't want any more whispering behind his back. He does understand that he's chosen to travel a bumpy, challenging road, but he's lucky to have a strong support system in place, particularly his wife and a few close friends. For him, this seems a good choice.

Finding Your Inspiration for Change

People interested in change often think about what they might do to improve their lives. How many times have you thought about losing weight or switching jobs or building a better relationship with your kids? How many times have you actually followed through with these ideas? If you're like most people, there is probably quite a large difference between what you think about doing and what you actually do. It's true that great achievements are the result of great ideas—but without action, ideas remain just that: ideas.

Deciding to gain control over drinking, substance use, or any other expression of addiction requires the same thought-into-action approach you need in order to accomplish anything, albeit on a much grander scale than the typical endeavor. Just ask Xavier. Now that he's made the decision to take some important steps toward an alcohol-and-gambling-free life, he realizes he'll need to do more than just think about what's required to make that happen. He needs to act!

Thinking about your motivation for change can help you translate thoughts into actions. Xavier has given a lot of thought to why he's choosing sobriety. He knows that his family will be happier and that he will have greater job security. He's tired of all the drama that drinking and gambling have brought into his life. He'd love to have more free time to build a better relationship with his kids, get to the gym, and maybe even start cooking again, something that was a passion of his before drinking and gambling monopolized all his free time. Keeping these motivators in mind is helping him stay focused and even excited about making the difficult changes that lie ahead.

What about you? What are your drivers for change? It's important to think about why you initially decided to make changes in your life, so that when there are bumps in the road of recovery—and there *will* be bumps along the way—you can recall your motivation and use it to continue moving forward. Remembering why you started the process of changing your life will help keep you focused and on track. So that your motivation for change is crystal clear in your mind, get out your journal and go through the following exercise.

1. List your reasons for wanting to change your gambling or substance use (or both). List as many reasons for change as come to mind.

2. Now circle the three most important reasons that are motivating you to seek change.

3. Make a copy of this list so that you can carry it with you at all times. Think of it as an important tool you can turn to whenever you're struggling with difficult choices about your substance use, gambling, or life in general. If there's ever a time when you feel as though you're ready to throw in the towel, look at this list; it will remind you of why you decided it was so important to change.

Integrating Change into Your Life

We covered goal setting extensively in Chapter Three. Goal setting goes hand in hand with motivation. If you think of motivation as point A or your starting point, then your goals are point B, where you'd like to wind up. Goals are integrally related to motivations, and they can often dovetail with one another.

As an example, an excerpt from a page in Xavier's journal appears on the following page. It's one of his first attempts at creating both short- and long-term goals to abstain from all of his addictions.

Xavier's journal entry includes his motivations as well as other thoughts and ideas he has for staying on track with his recovery. You might find it helpful to do some sort of goal-setting exercise in your efforts to recover. The most effective goals are what we refer to as SMART: specific, measurable, achievable, realistic, and time sensitive. You should have short-term stepping-stone goals that help you move in small, manageable increments toward your ultimate, long-term goals.

There are many useful points to take away from Xavier's journal entry. For example, he's given a few broad timelines and created a series of very concrete objectives for himself. He can make this process even more effective with a few adjustments. Instead of planning broad goals for one month and one year from now, he will concentrate for now on very specific goals to complete by the end of the week or even

August 14, 2011

I'm ready to make this change. I really don't have a choice because the thought of losing my family is unbearable. Maybe they can help . . . or maybe I should force myself to do this alone? No, I'll ask for help from my family and friends . . . I can do this. I'm ready!!

I need a preliminary long-term plan . . . So here is my list of goals:

Tomorrow

Assess. Reevaluate: Why is this process important?

*Note to self: Ask the kids how they feel about everything.

In 1 week

Besides wife/kids, pick 3 more people – invite to be part of my support group (check up on me, motivate, celebrate achievements)

*I will enlist Gianna's brother. He's easy to talk to, and I know he supports me.

In 1 month

Stay in office (away from bar) during the workday. No gambling during the workday.

*Evaluate how I'm feeling after work and on weekends. Schedule late meetings, dinners, etc., to keep myself occupied and distract urges to drink and gamble.

In 1 year

No drinking, gambling, or any sort of drug use at all.

*Ask family, few friends/support group over to dinner to discuss progress and reevaluate goals.

the end of the day. Writing down short-term, concrete, and attainable goals and completing them will give him a sense of accomplishment and make it easier to picture moving toward and completing larger goals. Xavier will become better and better at this process; because he's writing in his journal daily and accessing his goals often, he will refine these as he goes along. However, although refinement is key, you don't want to change your long-term goals too much or too often.

To help set your goals for your substance use and gambling, refer to the information in Chapter Three. There you'll find some sample goal sheets that will take you step-by-step through a detailed goal-setting process.

Analysis and Decision Making

Examining different situations that encourage you to use substances or to gamble and analyzing all aspects of your decision making, thoughts, and actions can be a very useful exercise. When you compare various situations that you've dealt with in the recent past, you often find similarities. Deconstructing these similarities will help identify triggers, patterns, and potential new strategies.

Using the Decision Chart we've provided, try this exercise. Keep your responses short, simple, and to the point. You don't need to write a novel but rather the what, when, and how of situations that have or could have triggered you to drink, drug, or gamble. Deconstructing these situations and all of the associated decisions will help you become more aware of your triggers and the justifications that you use to respond to these triggers. As you begin to recognize the situations and feelings that precede your substance use and gambling, you will be better equipped to manage any associated urges.

When Xavier uses this "tool for change," he uncovers a pattern of behavior he wasn't aware of before this. Looking at the chart, he sees that he tends to gamble when he's bored. When he feels this way, he usually makes the initial decision to go for a walk to clear his head;

Decision Chart

Use this chart to help deconstruct situations or patterns of behavior. Here are step-by-step instructions along with an example of how Xavier used the chart to analyze a situation where he bought scratch tickets.

1. In the first row, start by listing a substance use or other activity you wish to analyze. For example, in Xavier's case he might want to list "scratch tickets."
2. In the second row, Situation or Event, list where the substance use or activity takes place. Xavier writes "At work."
3. In the third row, Reason, Emotion, or Problem, briefly describe the influences that you believe encourage you to engage in this activity in this situation. After some thought, Xavier writes "Boredom" in this box.
4. In the row labeled Initial Decision, describe your initial thought that encouraged you to engage in the activity. Xavier writes that originally he intended to take a walk and, if he happened to pass a bodega along the way, then he would go in and buy some scratch tickets.
5. In the Justification row, list the reasoning behind your decision. Xavier justified his decision to go for a walk and subsequently buy the tickets by thinking "It was only a few" and, that if he won, the winnings would benefit his family.
6. Finally, in the last row, Decision, list the decision that guided your behavior. In this particular instance, Xavier's decision was to buy the scratch tickets.
7. Use the remaining columns to analyze additional activities. For instance, Xavier might also use this chart to analyze his drinking activities and whether stress or other emotions influence them.

Substance or Activity				
Situation or Event				
Reason, Emotion, or Problem				
Initial Decision				
Justification				
Decision				

if he just happens to pass a bodega, he'll run in and buy two or three scratch tickets. His justification for this is that it's just a couple of tickets, so what's the harm? And he could really win this time, which would benefit his family. His final decision quite often is to drop whatever he's doing to go buy scratch tickets.

Now that he's identified this pattern and even some of the reasons why it occurs, he can think about suitable alternatives. He can find more ways to engage in his work and family. Instead of going for a walk, he can get a snack, do a crossword puzzle, or head to the gym to blow off a little steam. All of these might help him avoid the end result of gambling.

Learning to Cope

Xavier now realizes that he often drinks and gambles because he's bored. These activities also help him manage stress when things get tense at the office or at home—or when he starts thinking about how much time and money he wastes on drinking and gambling. As Xavier repeatedly used drinking and gambling over the years to help relieve boredom and ease his distress, these activities became what we refer to as *coping strategies*. A coping strategy is anything you do to deal with and attempt to overcome your problems and difficulties. Granted, drinking and gambling aren't very productive, but they are coping strategies nonetheless.

To change his behavior and his coping style, Xavier has to do three things: (1) identify how he currently copes; (2) remember how he used to cope before he started drinking and gambling; and (3) come up with alternative ways of coping that have fewer negative consequences.

So what can he do to help change his ways? When he realizes he's bored, he can reach out to his wife or one of the other people who have pledged to offer support, go to the gym, do a crossword puzzle—or try any number of other coping mechanisms that don't carry such negative consequences.

Reversing the Direction of Your Thoughts

Your thoughts about events or situations and your interpretations of these situations can profoundly influence your reactions and your behaviors. Normally, this is not a problem. However, when automatic thoughts are consistently negative, frequent, and counterproductive for the situation, this way of thinking is a problem. We discuss the idea of automatic negative thoughts (ANTs) and their influence on your behavior at length in Chapter Five; you might find it helpful to go back and review this information.

Recognizing ANTs and guiding yourself to a more useful thought process can be especially helpful when dealing with substance abuse and any other expression of addiction, including gambling. Once you identify the thoughts that immediately jump into your mind when you're faced with a trigger for your substance use, you have an opportunity to reverse them. This can be a difficult skill to learn because it requires increased awareness of your substance use and gambling triggers as well as an understanding of how you specifically think and act after experiencing a trigger.

We hope that the previous sections that focused on analyzing your decisions and coping strategies have helped you learn more about your triggers and their consequences. Now we'll build on this by teaching you how to stop and reverse the thoughts that might accompany your undesirable behavior. Stopping and reversing automatic negative thoughts is a two-step process: first, you will need to identify your negative thoughts; second, you must learn to substitute alternative thoughts that are more rational and useful. The exercises in Chapter Five will help you practice these two steps. For now, remember that once you identify an automatic negative thought and the justification that supports it, you can evaluate the justification and, when you recognize that it is illogical, reverse it by substituting a more rational explanation. This new justification will not provide support for the automatic negative thought, and this reversal of justifications will let the thought pass.

Coping Chart

Complete this chart using these step-by-step instructions. We also provide Xavier's answers as an example.

1. In the first column, list the issue or emotion with which you are learning to cope. Xavier writes "boredom" as the emotion he is struggling with.
2. In the Past column, write down what you used to do before you began drinking, taking drugs, or gambling to cope with this issue. Xavier writes that he used to go to the gym, spend time with his friends and family, or cook his favorite dishes.
3. In the column labeled Present, write down what you do to cope with the issue now. Xavier writes "buy scratch tickets, play cards, and drink."
4. The Reflection column is for listing your thoughts about what changed that encouraged you to change your coping strategy and about how you think you might better cope in the future. In Xavier's case, he feels that gambling was more exciting than his old coping mechanisms and that drinking helped ease both boredom and stress. Going forward, he thinks he can begin spending time with friends and family and get to the gym more.
5. The final column, Future, is for you to list your new and improved coping strategy. Xavier will call his wife or another member of his support group when he feels bored and has an urge to drink or gamble. He's also renewed his gym membership and hired a personal trainer for sessions during a time of day he feels most susceptible to slipups.
6. Use the remaining rows to analyze additional issues with which you are learning to cope. For instance, Xavier also might do this same exercise for stress or anxiety.

Issue or Emotion	Past	Present	Reflection	Future
What is it that you need to cope with? What are the associated emotions?	*What did you do to change this feeling before your addiction?*	*What do you do to change this feeling now?*	*What is different now? What are alternative ways to cope?*	*What do you need to do to use these alternative coping methods?*

For example, what uncomfortable experiences will you have if you act impulsively in response to a trigger? What might you gain by coping with the trigger differently and changing your response to it? When Xavier tries this exercise, he focuses on the fact that he gets bored, especially at work, and this often leads him to the very behaviors he's trying to change. But now that he understands this, he's sometimes able to reverse his justifications for drinking and gambling and even replace them with a more productive line of thinking. Little by little, Xavier finds other things to think about besides drinking and gambling. There are many events and important people in his life; focusing on them helps Xavier gently manage his triggers and urges so that he maintains control of his behavior in a desirable direction.

Thought reversal can work if you take it to heart. When you find yourself in the middle of a triggering situation, try to use the material you produced during the exercises in deconstructing situations and coping to imagine how you might act. When you start to justify your negative thoughts using old and usual habits, stop. Attempt to reverse your thoughts by making a new decision based on a new justification.

The Physical and Mental Aspects of Change

If, like Xavier, you find that stress, tension, or feeling overwhelmed is what sometimes leads to your substance use or gambling, then discovering ways to calm down and relax can help you moderate or abstain from these patterns. The point of relaxation exercises is to take the energy from your urges and redirect it. Intense concentration on specific aspects of your body might help you learn focusing skills that can enable you to manage triggers and keep them from distracting you as you work toward your goals. Relaxed muscles and breathing, for example, are incompatible with the experience of stress. Try the exercises we've detailed in this chapter as well the additional relaxation exercises in Chapter Five.

Calming Breath

When you feel stressed, agitated, anxious, or just generally tense, paying attention to your breathing can help calm your nerves. Paying attention means tuning in to the breaths of air you take in (inhaling) and the air that you breathe out (exhaling).

As you sit reading this book now, pay attention to your breathing. Focus on the smell, the temperature, and the path of the air as it travels from your nose to your lungs. Think about how quickly you normally breathe and how that reflects your mental state. Generally, you take deeper, slower breaths when you feel more relaxed; these breaths use your lungs and your diaphragm, which is a thick, muscle-like sheet under your rib cage that pushes your chest cavity upward and outward. When you feel nervous or anxious, your breathing usually becomes shallower; it's quick, and uses only the upper parts of your chest cavity. This kind of breathing can lead to hyperventilation because it fails to allow enough oxygen to get to your brain. This is the reason you feel lightheaded when you breathe too fast.

Now that you've focused on your normal breathing pattern, try this *calming breath* exercise. Find a quiet spot and limit distractions, such as your cell phone, e-mail, or TV. If you want, close your eyes as you do this. When you become more practiced, you can use calming breaths in virtually any situation. As you do this exercise, notice the distinctive feelings associated with different types of breathing.

1. Start by taking five deep, slow breaths. When doing this, any tightness, such as raising your shoulders or pressing your lips together, are signs of tension; we want to avoid that kind of breathing in this exercise. With each deep breath, you should feel your chest rise and expand.
2. Now take five slow but ordinary breaths. With these breaths, you should still avoid tightness. However, focus on your chest again; the muscle movement should feel the same as that of a deep breath.

3. Next take three quick breaths. It's important not to take too many quick breaths, as this may cause you to hyperventilate.
4. Finally take a deep breath, hold it for fifteen seconds, and then let all the air out.

Meditation

Meditation is one of the oldest forms of relaxation. It includes skills associated with both muscle relaxation (which you learned in Chapter Five) and the previous breathing exercise. The added element to meditation is mental clarity. Meditation helps clear your mind of your triggers and other distractions, if only for a moment.

The mental emptiness of meditation is temporary, but the effects can be cumulative and long lasting. When you meditate, you often focus on a word, a phrase, or an object. As you maintain this focused attention, you let the thoughts and feelings that enter your mind pass as if you were watching a movie, except that you do not react; you simply watch passively. People who meditate learn gradually to let things go rather than reacting.

Try this simple beginner's meditation. Start by sitting in a quiet place and repeatedly and softly saying a chosen phrase out loud until you start to feel more relaxed. (Xavier has chosen to say "I do it all out of love.") As you gradually begin to tune out distractions, such as dogs barking, cars honking, and doors squeaking, begin to repeat your phrase only in your mind, and now focus on your breathing. Let each breath and each repetition of the phrase represent a release of the negative energy that both gambling and substance use have brought into your life. Each time that you meditate, imagine that you are releasing the negative energy from a future urge and continuing your journey on the road to change.

Meditation doesn't have to take your whole day. As you progress, you will be able to complete a session in ten to twenty minutes. The more you practice, the more your self-awareness will progress and the better you will become at recognizing and managing stress and tension.

This is just one example of how to meditate. There are many types and schools of meditation. If you find it helpful and would like to gain a deeper understanding of this relaxation method, you can take classes, buy guided meditations on CD, or download one into your MP3 player.

When you first begin the process of recovery, it might seem as though there are many obstacles preventing you from getting better. But if you stop and really think about it, many of these hurdles might not be quite as difficult to overcome as you first thought; some barriers might actually help you in the long run. However, if you find that you're not improving, don't get discouraged. Self-help exercises might not be sufficient to reduce your symptoms right now. If this is the case, consider seeking professional help, as we discuss in the following section.

Attempting to Change with Professional Help

Marion was a rebellious teen who started drinking and smoking pot while in high school. She's been smoking and drinking almost daily ever since, now, in her late twenties, she's added cocaine to the mix. She also gambles on a regular basis, usually going to the track or making the rounds of card games at various local bars and clubs. Most of her personal and professional relationships are in a shambles. Her parents told her they won't help bail her out of her latest financial crisis, so she's found herself saddled with some serious money issues too.

Over the years, she's occasionally tried to quit her drinking, drugging, and gambling, but she's never made a serious effort to clean up her act until now. She's disturbed that she owes money to a cocaine dealer while her gambling debts are also beginning to pile up. All this has opened her eyes to how serious her problems have become.

Marion's family has pretty much written her off; consequently, even though she's finally ready to make real improvements, she doesn't feel she has a good deal of personal support this time around. She desperately wants to have a better life, but she feels judged and isolated by her friends and family. It seems as if there is no one to turn to and no one to talk to. She feels she needs help in her recovery, but it's not going to come from her loved ones.

As Marion has found, sometimes changing on your own is difficult. But it's important to understand that reaching out and asking for help is not a negative reflection on your determination to change. Rather, it is a reflection of the power that gambling and substance use can hold over you. If you've implemented some or all of the various strategies we've discussed in this and other chapters and still find yourself struggling with the issues that brought you to this book, seeking professional help can be a very productive move indeed. Even if this is your first pass at recovery, if you don't feel strong enough to travel the road yourself, there is no shame in seeking help.

In Marion's case, because she's alienated much of her personal support system, she starts her recovery journey by going to a psychotherapist, who works with her to create a treatment program that specifically deals with both her substance abuse and her gambling.

The therapist she chose happens to be a social worker, who, like all good professional counselors, has spent years learning about personal problems, suffering, and how to change behavior patterns. Marion does wish she had more backing from those close to her, but she's thankful that her new therapist possesses the skills and resources to help her. She feels that with his help, perhaps she can get to the point where her life will improve enough to convince her friends and family that she's serious about change. Maybe then they'll be able to rally behind her and champion her recovery.

Marion's therapist has encouraged her to use many of the self-help strategies we've discussed earlier in this chapter to reinforce what they discuss in session. He also suggested that she attend regular Alcoholics Anonymous and Gamblers Anonymous meetings for additional support.

Initially Marion was hesitant to go to meetings because she lives in a small town. She's afraid word will get around, sullying her reputation even further and making it even more difficult to clean up her relationships and get her career on track. Her therapist has explained that the meetings are completely confidential; all of the attendees are or have been in the same or a very similar situation, so the atmosphere tends to be one of mutual respect; everyone who attends has made a promise to keep the sessions private. Because Marion craves moral support and a shoulder to lean on, her therapist feels that attending regular group meetings can reinforce her therapeutic work. He's right. She's draws a lot of strength and inspiration from her daily meetings.

Social workers, psychologists, psychiatrists, and group leaders have varying degrees of professional training, but all the good ones have the skills and knowledge to work with you to design a treatment program that will target your substance use and gambling-related problems. If you're interested in getting this type of professional help, your health care provider, insurance provider, local emergency room, human resources department at work, or clergy are often the best places to start looking for referrals. There is also plenty of information about local self-help groups and therapists who specialize in dealing with addiction to be found on the Web and in the yellow pages.

Marion's therapist sent her to a physician to discuss at length the idea of alcohol withdrawal. Although no one knows all of the mechanisms that trigger substance use or gambling problems, research has shown that genetic predispositions and chemical changes in the brain play important roles. Some people therefore have trouble getting through the detoxification phase of recovery without some type of medication. Ultimately, Marion and her recovery team decided this was not the case for her, but it does seem particularly useful for many others who go through nicotine and other stimulant withdrawal as well as for those who withdraw from alcohol or other sedatives.

The decision to take medication requires a thoughtful discussion with an addiction treatment specialist. This type of professional is usually a licensed physician, psychiatrist, psychologist, or social worker. Currently, there are only a few medications that are specifically used to treat substance abuse. Naltrexone (Vivitrol) and acamprosate (Campral) are sometimes used as part of a treatment program for alcohol or gambling addiction; physicians sometimes prescribe methadone, naltrexone, and buprenorphine for heroin addiction or addiction to other opioid drugs.

Marion has found one treatment obstacle particularly challenging: the fact that her insurance plan won't cover all of her therapy sessions. Thankfully, she hasn't let this deter her from her goals. She had a confidential meeting with someone in her human resources department at work to help negotiate a reduced rate with her counselor until they can find an appropriate insurance solution; the company was also able to provide her with additional low- and no-cost resources. Because Marion was ready to change, she didn't give up or let any obstacles stand in her way. She's been sober for almost one year now and feels a new sense of hopefulness. She noticed these changes after only a couple of months, but her new sense of self is growing and becoming more stable as she approaches her first anniversary of sobriety. She's got a newfound sense of purpose that motivates her to get up and do her best every day.

WHERE DO YOU GO FROM HERE?

Perhaps you have chosen a single pathway to recovery or put together aspects of different pathways that best suit your needs. Or maybe you're not ready to choose a pathway yet. If so, that's not a problem. You don't have to feel rushed to make a decision. If you are not ready for change now, this does not mean that you will never be interested in change. Most likely, you will be ready for change at a later time.

We do hope that the main takeaway from this chapter is that you can indeed recover from both substance abuse and gambling. It requires a lot of hard work on your part, but once you start the process, you'll see that it's worth the effort. Everyone deserves to have a better life. Choosing recovery can help you get to a better place.

Part 3

How to
Stay the
Course

9 Preventing Relapses

What you'll learn in this chapter: Relapses are often part of the process of recovery from addiction. This chapter antici- pates such common episodes. You'll learn why you have backslides and slipups, and we'll give you strategies for getting back on track when you do go off course.

The road to behavior change or recovery from any type of addic- tion is rarely straight and smooth. Most people find recovery full of unexpected twists and turns, so it is important to be ready for these situations. Even when you have the best intentions and give it your best effort, you might find yourself backsliding into your old ways. Up to 90 percent of people who are in the process of overcoming addiction "slip up" at some point during the first year of recovery. When you revert back to your old behavior for a short period of time—just one or two episodes—we refer to it as a *lapse*. If your return to problematic behavior is more long term, we refer to it as a *relapse*.

You can lapse or relapse even when you've done well up to that point and think the worst is behind you. And when you do stumble, it can feel like falling off a cliff. Many people have nightmares about lapses and wake up relieved to know it was only a dream. When a lapse really happens, it can be devastating. Relapses in particular can leave you with a deep sense of frustration. No one wants to feel

SORTING OUT AND CONFRONTING MULTIPLE EXPRESSIONS OF ADDICTION

Your risk for a relapse increases when you are attempting to cope with more than one issue at a time. One of the best strategies for recovering from multiple expressions of addiction and the many issues that often accompany addiction is to set goals for each and create a schedule that devotes time to managing each individual problem. For example, if you suffer from anxiety, work with some of the tools specifically designed for managing anxiety that are laid out in Chapter Five. To control gambling, work with the strategies in Chapter Four. To address your issues with drinking or substance abuse, rely on the strategies detailed in Chapter Eight. Keeping your other problems under control might be a key to successfully changing your gambling; alternatively, gambling might be the key to better managing other behaviors. It's true that maintaining your control of everything will require a great deal of attention, planning, and hard work. Your coping skills will be tested. There's no getting around this fact. Keep practicing and remember: the outcome is worth the effort.

as though she's destroyed all the good she's done or the goals she's worked so hard to achieve.

The truth is, slipups are part of the recovery process. You haven't failed if you have a lapse or a relapse. In fact, they can be a useful part of your overall progress toward change and have the potential to help you learn more about yourself and grow as a person. With effort and planning, you can work through them and successfully continue on with your recovery.

One of the big unknowns about the recovery process is whether there is ever a point when you're truly safe from relapse. Because emotions, behaviors, and thought patterns can be so ingrained, it's hard to say how long you'll have to stay fully engaged and on top of your recovery. You probably wonder if there will ever be a time when you can relax and let your guard down.

There aren't any simple answers. Everyone is different. Some people need to maintain a diligent attitude toward recovery for years, perhaps even for the rest of their lives, taking care to manage what they think, feel, and do much of the time. Others seem to find the process easier and, as a result, might be more casual about how they manage their recovery once they progress past the initial phases. Typically, people who are struggling with addiction—whether their issue is drinking, drugging, gambling, shopping, or eating—must continue to monitor their behavior even after they have gained control. The same is true for someone who has struggled with a problematic thought or emotional pattern, such as excessive anxiety, extreme mood swings, or compulsive behavior. Experts and people recovering from addiction alike often refer to the "One day at a time" mantra because it is so apropos to making and sustaining change.

You may recall Gary from Chapter Four. Gary had a problem with betting on sporting events, particularly football games. For years he was unable to get his gambling under control. Once he decided to change, he worked hard and employed many of the strategies we've detailed throughout this book and, as a result, he's now abstained from gambling for more than four years. It's been a happy four years: he's rebuilt personal relationships, cleaned up his debt, and moved forward in a positive way with his life.

One day, Gary's boss asked him to attend a training program that was scheduled to run a full month. Agreeing to attend put Gary under a great deal of stress. He'd have to put in some extra hours to keep up with his usual workload, but completing the training would position him for a big promotion. Gary was excited about the opportunity and flattered that his boss had chosen him—yet he also could feel his stomach churning with anxiety. What if he couldn't live up to expectations?

As he sat through the workshops day after day, he was surprised to realize that, in addition to his worry, he also felt bored. The leader used no visual aids and droned on and on in a monotonous voice. For the first time in a long while, Gary felt his mind wandering toward gambling. He began to feel his old urges bubble up to the surface, and these urges felt just as strong as ever.

UNDERSTANDING TRIGGERS

A lapse or relapse doesn't happen in a vacuum. Something has to happen. During recovery, the person, place, or thing that leads to a relapse is a *trigger*. And handling triggers is one of the fundamental skills you'll need to learn if you want your recovery to be successful in both the long and short terms.

Triggers tend to fall into two categories: those you can avoid and those you can't. You can avoid walking into a casino, sitting down at a table, and staring at a high-stakes poker game. You can't avoid all advertisements for in-person or online poker games, all movies that show scenes of gambling, and all social occasions where there might be a friendly game going on in a corner. With the former type of situation, you have complete control; with the latter, the best you can do is limit exposure and build up your resistance to such triggers, because in the real world there will always be a time, place, or situation where you might come face-to-face with a trigger.

If your trigger for gambling is a particular grocery store that sells lottery tickets, you might avoid that grocery store. But you also can prepare yourself by developing specific strategies for managing that particular trigger. For example, you could begin to shop for groceries elsewhere, schedule your visits for the time of day when the lottery window is closed, or take someone shopping with you to provide additional support. (See Chapter Three to review goal setting and Chapter Six to review scheduling.)

WHAT ARE YOUR TRIGGERS?

It's helpful to think through carefully exactly what your triggers are for every issue from which you are trying to recover. In the past, Gary found that listing all of his problematic activities plus their potential triggers helped control relapses. For example, he recalls from work he's previously done that worry and boredom are two of his greatest gambling triggers.

If you feel that you're in danger of backsliding, list in your journal all the issues, thoughts, emotions, and addictive behaviors from which you are trying to recover. Then list what you think might be your potential triggers. Triggers can be thoughts, situations, moods, objects, people, or anything else. If it causes an urge or temptation to bubble up, then consider it a trigger.

Addictive Behaviors	Trigger(s)
_____	_____
_____	_____
_____	_____

UNDERSTANDING SLIPUPS

Even the strongest, most determined person is susceptible to a lapse or relapse. In this section, we'll explore some of the major reasons for them, including common thought processes and emotions that might leave you vulnerable to slipups, along with some suggested strategies for preventing, eliminating, and recovering from them.

Lack of Inner Confidence

Despite staying clean and sober and avoiding card games for more than six months, Caroline did not feel great about herself. Rather than focusing on the accomplishment of recovery, she beat herself up on a daily basis for all the years she'd spent drinking and gambling. Why was everything so hard for her, she wondered, yet seemingly so easy for other people? Why did bad things always seem to come her way? In a particularly low moment, she poured herself a drink and placed several bets at the local off-track betting parlor.

Caroline lacks inner confidence—what clinicians refer to as *self-efficacy*. People who don't have a strong sense of self-efficacy tend to have trouble focusing, directing, and therefore managing their behavior; they find it hard to resist the temptations that can divert their attention and lead to troublesome behavior. They often lack discipline and, as a result, have difficulty balancing their lives. When the going gets a little rough, they struggle to stick with their recovery plans and have difficulty staying in balance and in control.

Low self-efficacy often fills a person's head with disorganized and sometimes negative thoughts they can't seem to shake or counterbalance. During recovery, they feel that they don't have enough willpower to succeed or that they are failures for getting themselves into such a predicament in the first place. They often feel that they never really can change. These negative thoughts and feelings have one thing in common: they are too simple to explain away a lapse. Rarely do lapses result for just one reason. Rather, they're usually the product of a long chain of events, thoughts, feelings, and situations.

Self-Pity

Negative thoughts aside, people who have minimal self-belief often feel sorry for themselves. Whether it rained that day or she missed the train, Caroline tends to blow these things out of proportion. They don't just happen: they happen to *her*. She feels that life isn't fair, and she doesn't understand why she is so powerless.

One strategy for helping to build self-efficacy is to counteract automatic negative thoughts (ANTs) with more rational and reasonable responses. Chapter Five provides a detailed description of how to do this. In a nutshell, constant negative thoughts that involuntarily pop into your head can erode your belief system. Learning to substitute positive, rational thoughts for negative thoughts can help you build resilience and a more positive attitude.

Caroline, for instance, might do much better if she came to accept the belief that the train did not leave without her for the express purpose of ruining her day and that even though she missed the train,

---

COMMON AUTOMATIC NEGATIVE THOUGHTS AND RATIONAL RESPONSES

Negative Thought	Rational Response
I don't have enough willpower.	Willpower alone cannot change a negative behavior pattern: change is a complex process that requires skills.
I am a failure.	Your expectations for recovery are unreasonably high. Reevaluate your goals and remember that lapses and relapses often are part of recovery. You are moving along the path to change.
I can never change.	Everyone changes. You just need to find the right combination of skills and resources to guide your change in the direction you want it to go.
I feel guilty and ashamed.	There is nothing shameful about trying to have a different kind of life. A lapse is simply part of this change process. Lapses are bumps in the road; bumps sometimes hurt.

her day still might be just fine after all. (See Common Automatic Negative Thoughts and Rational Responses.)

Self-efficacy and confidence are valuable assets during recovery. The stronger your belief that you can maintain your change, stick with your coping strategies, and meet your objectives, the more likely this is to be true. High self-efficacy is a powerful tool for avoiding relapse. It is much more empowering to view yourself as someone who bravely and proactively faces down his or her problems and deals with them decisively than as someone who has no control over what happens and simply lets events unfold.

Ambivalence

Ambivalence refers to uncertainty or indecision about which course to follow. Ambivalence is about wanting and not wanting something at the same time. Some people are ambivalent about their recovery because they're afraid to fail. Others are afraid to succeed. Still others are afraid of both success and failure. These fears reflect the struggle between the motivation to change and the idea that recovery will have adverse consequences—for example, added responsibility and accountability.

Harry is a textbook case of someone who is of two minds about his recovery from both gambling and depression. On the one hand, it's a relief to be free of the heaviness of his moods and the financial burden of his gambling losses. On the other hand, he's now faced with the emotionally challenging task of trying to repair all the damage he's done to his personal relationships. He's grateful for the improvements in his life, but sometimes he thinks that it might be easier to remain a depressed gambler.

Who can say what will happen once you stop negative behaviors and start taking steps to turn your life around? For some people, the uncertainty is too much to bear, and it seems easier and safer to leave things as they are, even if their current situation is much less than ideal. Some people can get past this feeling for a time, but then they slide into a relapse because they begin to think they can handle their addiction or negative behaviors better this time around.

Ambivalence is a central issue for people trying to make changes in their lives. Sometimes people both want and don't want the same thing. When ambivalence is painful, it puts you at risk for relapse. The pain of ambivalent feelings often causes people to erase one side of the contradictory feeling. Consequently, painful ambivalence often leaves people with only one side of an issue, so they become hesitant to act, and wind up treading water in the same old place. When you permit yourself to feel ambivalent, even though it can be uncomfortable, that feeling can be a catalyst for change because it allows for the other side of an issue to emerge. This can energize you to do something about your situation rather than leave things as they are.

Harry wants to continue to curtail his gambling, but he's tempted to start again because it helped him avoid emotionally charged issues. For many years, his ambivalence allowed him to justify the high cost of his self-destructive behavior. But when the positive perceptions of quitting finally seemed to outweigh the negative ones, it motivated him toward recovery. Is it worth giving in to the temptation, he wonders?

Having ambivalent feelings toward recovery is perfectly natural. Despite the natural tendency to suppress these feelings, try not to. Instead, share your feelings with your friends, family, and anyone you consider part of your support system. They're more likely to be happy that you've shared your feelings with them than be disappointed in you for having them; and the chances are that you'll feel stronger and more resolved to move forward with your change after talking things out.

Recovering from addiction does not always follow a direct path. If you do slip up—whether in the short or long term—it can be tough to get back on track again. The slip might magnify your ambivalence. You might feel as though you've been knocked back to square one, and if you've put a lot of effort into your recovery, it can be discouraging to feel as though you're starting over. These feelings are normal. Remember, just because you've faltered doesn't mean you've failed. Similarly, setbacks along the road to change do not mean that recovery isn't worth it.

After a lapse or relapse, it might help to focus on the advantages of meeting your long-term goals as a reminder of why you started this journey in the first place. What were your reasons for wanting to change your life? How much did your negative behaviors interfere with your life, and how much more do you accomplish when you stop them? How much happier are you when your negative behaviors and addiction are under control? Keeping the answers to these questions in mind can help erase the doubts and ambivalence you feel about recovery and allow you to concentrate on your ultimate goals.

Coping with Stress and Challenging Situations

Daya has trouble dealing with even minor setbacks, and this contributed to her excessive drinking and gambling in the first place. She's made a real effort to improve her life by using many of the self-help techniques we've talked about in this book, and she did quite well for several months. But then her mother was diagnosed with cancer. Her first reaction when she got the news was to reach for the bottle and buy a handful of lottery tickets.

Having effective coping strategies in place is an important way to avoid falling back into old patterns of behavior. Without effective coping skills, it's difficult to stand up to life's challenges. Yes, finding out that your mother has cancer can be devastating news, but if Daya had already established some solid coping mechanisms, she'd be better able to resist the urge to drink and gamble.

Everyone experiences at least some stress. How you deal with problems is what affects your risk of relapse. Daya, for instance, doesn't have many friends or any hobbies, so when she learned of her mother's illness, she had no one to talk to and no outlet for her tension other than gambling and drinking. So it's not surprising that she lapsed as a way of dealing with bad news. Gambling and drinking give her the illusion that her life is balanced and provide stress relief in the short term; the reality is that they'll most likely cause more problems for her over the long term.

What might be helpful for someone like Daya is to cultivate some replacement activities. She might, for instance, head to the gym and burn off some steam on the treadmill, or take a class after work where she can engage her mind and meet some new people. Then she'd have social alternatives to gambling and drinking whenever she feels the pressure in her life rising. These activities might not necessarily dampen her urges, but at least she'd have something positive in her life to help pull her through the rough patches.

Other useful coping strategies include goal setting (which you learned in Chapter Three), scheduling (Chapter Six), and monitoring your urges and triggers (Chapter Four). These all can help you manage your urges or at least make resisting the urges less of a burden.

Interestingly, too much of a good thing can be its own form of stress. Like sad or difficult times, happy times can increase your chances of a lapse or relapse. Getting married, graduating from school, or receiving a promotion are classic examples of "good stress." Although positive and happy, these events have a way of encouraging people to make a good situation even better. You might, for instance, feel that it's OK to toast a wedding with Champagne, go on a shopping spree for new clothes when you graduate, or celebrate a promotion with a night out at a casino. Overconfidence can increase the danger of letting go of your vigilance on happy occasions. In situations like this, it's easy to forget about trying to manage your behavior, but it's just as important to keep working your strategies for change and resisting your urges. Good times can go bad quickly, and you can slide into a lapse before you realize what's happening.

Remember too that you can't control everything and everyone. People you know sometimes get angry, feel disappointed, or don't have faith in your recovery. You might have an argument with your partner, not get invited to a family function, or have a gambling buddy who's not yet ready to lose you as a partner; in each of these situations, people who care about you might inadvertently sabotage your efforts to change. You might go to a wedding with an open bar or attend an office party where the theme is casino night. These scenarios can be very challenging and will open you to temptation, and they will be particularly difficult if you didn't anticipate them. But if your coping strategies are firmly in place, you have a better chance of navigating them successfully.

One thing you want to avoid is intentionally testing the boundaries by, for example, going to a bar and ordering a fruit juice or attending a card game but not joining in. The idea of testing is common among people recovering from addiction, but it's not a good one. Unless you are deliberately creating an exposure as we describe in Chapter Five, why tempt fate? There are plenty of times in life when you'll be tested without putting yourself in harm's way on purpose.

Taking Recovery for Granted

You might experience a relapse even though you've been feeling better about managing your impulses. Sam, whom you'll read about in the next section, hadn't gambled for more than six months before he ran into a few guys he knew from the poker tables, which triggered a lapse as if out of nowhere. If you had asked him about his recovery the day before that chance meeting—even an hour before—he would have told you how good it felt not to gamble and how much he enjoyed having his life back. He let his guard down and got lax about his recovery strategies.

Just because you start feeling better doesn't mean you can stop using all the strategies you learned from working through this book. No matter how strong you feel, you must maintain a lifestyle balance and the exercises that sustain this balance.

DEALING WITH A SLIPUP

How you interpret a lapse is probably the most important factor in what happens next. For example, Sam struggled with gambling for more than a decade before he finally decided to change his life. By using many of the self-help strategies laid out in the previous chapters, he was able to curtail his gambling for more than six months before he ran into some of his old gambling buddies at a restaurant one night and then spent the next few days playing cards with them. Ultimately he stopped gambling for some reasons he understood—and some he didn't. But what's next for Sam?

Sam now has two basic choices. He can think of this lapse into gambling as a defeat, give up, and plunge into a total relapse. Or he can look at it as a learning experience. He can ask himself what contributed to the lapse and what he can do to prevent another one in the future. He can think about his motivation for giving into temptation and, going forward, what might make him less vulnerable when he is in the same situation.

WHAT'S YOUR RELAPSE SCENARIO?

What would it take for you to relapse? Imagine a situation that might trigger a relapse. Focus on various aspects of this situation: your mood, events going on in your life that might make you vulnerable, your response to this situation, whom you are with, how these people make you feel, and anything else you think might contribute to this imaginary relapse. Now make a plan for how you will cope with this situation. Set plans as you would a goal. The more you practice this, the more likely you will follow through on your plan when the actual situation arises.

The chart here formally asks the same types of questions that Sam asks of himself. Whenever you've had a lapse or feel one coming on, it's useful to have the answers to these questions. The simple act of jotting the answers down and then pulling them out during times of temptation can provide a certain amount of protection against future lapses.

Lapse	
Circumstances where and when lapse occurred	
Likely triggers	
Thoughts and emotions	
What can I do to prevent future lapses?	

Sam's experience taught him that he is most vulnerable to a lapse when faced with an unexpected trigger—in this case, a random encounter with some old gambling buddies. When you have no immediate plan in place for dealing with such a scenario, it's like working a trapeze without a net. You might navigate the situation successfully, but what if you don't? If you find yourself in such a predicament, here are three instant coping strategies you can try:

- **Leave the situation.** Immediately remove yourself from the triggering circumstance. Sometimes this will seem abrupt and rude, but that's OK. In Sam's case, he could have made an excuse about being late for an appointment and beat a quick exit. Perhaps his buddies would have been confused or even a little hurt. However, Sam would have avoided a lapse.
- **Delay acting on the trigger.** Force yourself to wait before taking action. For instance, Sam could have told the guys to go on ahead and that he'd meet up with them later. This would have bought him some time to think through whether or not he really wanted to gamble. He'd also have a moment to employ some of his self-help strategies to help dampen his urge to gamble.
- **Think on your feet.** You can quickly deconstruct the situation and come up with a plan for dealing with it. This requires fast thinking and some wherewithal, but it can be done. Sam, for instance, might have seen that his gambling buddies were in the restaurant before they spotted him. He could have left quietly without saying hello, thereby preventing the meeting in the first place.

Whether you avoid the lapse or not, once you have discovered a red flag, you have the power to avoid it in the future. If he's really serious about maintaining his recovery, Sam now knows to steer clear of the restaurant where his poker buddies hang out.

WHERE DO YOU GO FROM HERE?

In this chapter, we discussed the common reasons for lapses and relapses in order to increase your awareness of some factors that are often associated with reverting back to old behaviors. To counter the potential harm of lapses and relapses, we also discussed some strategies for interpreting them. If you slip up in some way or are concerned that you might, please consider rereading this chapter as well as any other parts of this book that you think will be useful for staying on track or getting you back on your pathway to change.

Resources and Further Reading

Here we've provided a list of further reading and resources should you wish to pursue information beyond what we've included in this book. This is by no means an exhaustive list of materials and organizations aimed at helping problem gamblers. However, we're satisfied that it represents a wide scope of credible and high-quality resources. We recommend you also check state and local listings for additional resources in your area.

Books and Articles

Brenner, R., & Brenner, B. A. (1990). *Gambling and speculation: A theory, a history, and a future of some human decisions.* Cambridge: Cambridge University Press.

Clotfelter, C. T., & Cook, P. J. (1989). *Selling hope: State lotteries in America.* Cambridge, MA: Harvard University Press.

Custer, R. L., & Milt, H. (1985). *When luck runs out: Help for compulsive gamblers and their families.* New York: Warner Books.

Denizet-Lewis, B. (2009). *America anonymous: Eight addicts in search of a life.* New York: Simon & Schuster.

Fleming, A. M. (1978). *Something for nothing: A history of gambling.* New York: Delacorte Press.

Horvath, T. A. (1998). *Sex, drugs, gambling, & chocolate: A workbook for overcoming addictions.* San Louis Obispo, CA: Impact.

Khantzian, E. J., & Albanese, M. J. (2008). *Understanding addiction as self medication: Finding hope behind the pain.* Lanham, MD: Rowman & Littlefield.

Ladouceur, R., Sylvain, C., Boutin, C., & Doucet, C. (2002). *Understanding and treating the pathological gambler.* West Sussex, England: Wiley.

Lears, T.J.J. (2003). *Something for nothing: Luck in America.* New York: Viking.

Lesieur, H. R. (1977). *The chase: Career of the compulsive gambler.* Garden City, NY: Anchor Press.

National Endowment for Financial Education and National Council on Problem Gambling. (2000). *Personal financial strategies for the loved ones of problem gamblers.* Denver, CO: National Endowment for Financial Education.

Orford, J. (1985). *Excessive appetites: A psychological view of addictions.* Hoboken, NJ: Wiley.

Prochaska, J. O., Norcross, J. C., & DiClemente, C. C. (1994). *Changing for good: A revolutionary six-stage program for overcoming bad habits and moving your life positively forward.* New York: Avon.

Shaffer, H. J., Hall, M. N., Vander Bilt, J., & George, E. (Eds.). (2003). *Futures at stake: Youth, gambling and society.* Reno: University of Nevada Press.

Shaffer, H. J., & Jones, S. B. (1989). *Quitting cocaine: The struggle against impulse.* Lexington, MA.: Lexington Books.

Shaffer, H. J., & Korn, D. A. (2002). Gambling and related mental disorders: A public health analysis. *Annual Review of Public Health, 23,* 171–212. Palo Alto, CA: Annual Reviews.

Shaffer, H. J., LaPlante, D. A., LaBrie, R. A., Kidman, R. C., Donato, A. N., & Stanton, M. V. (2004). Toward a syndrome model of addiction: Multiple expressions, common etiology. *Harvard Review of Psychiatry, 12,* 367–374.

Shaffer, H. J., & Martin, R. (2011). Disordered gambling: Etiology, trajectory, and clinical considerations. *Annual Review of Clinical Psychology, 7,* 483–510. doi: 10.1146/annurev-clinpsy-040510-143928.

Shaffer, H. J., Stein, S., Gambino, B., & Cummings, T. N. (Eds.). (1989). *Compulsive gambling: Theory, research and practice.* Lexington, MA: Lexington Books.

Zinberg, N. E. (1984). *Drug, set, and setting: The basis for controlled intoxicant use.* New Haven, CT: Yale University Press.

Self-Help Fellowships

Gamblers Anonymous
International Service Office
PO Box 17173
Los Angeles, CA 90017
Phone: (213) 386-8789
Fax: (213) 386-0030
Web site: www.gamblersanonymous.org/

Gamblers Anonymous (GA) is a 12-step self-help group modeled after Alcoholics Anonymous. GA describes itself as a fellowship of men and women who share their experience, strength, and hope with each other so that they may solve their common problem and help others recover from a gambling problem. The only requirement for membership is a desire to stop gambling. There are no dues or fees for GA membership, as it self-supports through contributions. The organization is not allied with any sect, denomination, politics, organization, or institution. Its primary purpose is to help their members stop gambling. Its Web site contains information and links to various state and local chapters and meetings.

Gam-Anon
International Service Office
PO Box 157
Whitestone, NY 11357
Phone: (718) 352-1671
Fax: (718) 746-2571
Web site: www.gam-anon.org/

Gam-Anon describes itself as a fellowship of men and women who have been affected by a gambling problem. Thus meetings are often attended by the loved ones of those with gambling problems. Gam-Anon meetings aim to provide new insight into what can be a devastating problem in many people's lives. Its Web site includes a list of local chapters and meetings.

Resource Organizations

Division on Addiction
Cambridge Health Alliance
an affiliate of Harvard Medical School
Station Landing
101 Station Landing, 2nd Floor
Medford, MA 02155
Phone: (781) 306-8600
Web site: www.divisiononaddictions.org/
E-mail: info@divisiononaddictions.org

The mission of the Division on Addiction (the Division) at the Cambridge Health Alliance, a Harvard Medical School teaching affiliate, is to strengthen worldwide understanding of addiction through innovative research, education, and the global exchange of information. The ultimate goal of the Division is to alleviate the social, medical, and economic burdens caused by addictive behaviors.

National Center for Responsible Gaming
1299 Pennsylvania Avenue, NW, Suite 1175
Washington, DC 20004
Phone: (202) 552-2689
Fax: (202) 552-2676
Web site: www.ncrg.org
E-mail: info@ncrg.org

The National Center for Responsible Gaming (NCRG) is the only national organization exclusively devoted to funding research that helps increase understanding of pathological and youth gambling and find effective methods of treatment for the disorder. The NCRG is the American Gaming Association's affiliated charity.

National Council on Problem Gambling
730 11th Street, NW, Suite 601
Washington, DC 20001
Phone: (202) 547-9204
Web site: www.ncpgambling.org
E-mail: ncpg@ncpgambling.org

The National Council on Problem Gambling (NCPG) and its thirty-three state affiliates have a variety of gambling-related resources available through their Web site, including information about national certification conducted by the National Gambling Counseling Certification Board; a search feature for locating nationally certified counselors; and a list of scheduled continuing education unit courses and resources. In addition, the NCPG operates a confidential twenty-four-hour, toll-free helpline at (800) 522-4700.

Responsible Gambling Organization of Canada
www.responsiblegambling.org

The Responsible Gambling Organization of Canada offers research information and abstracts on current articles about problem gambling in the United States, Canada, and abroad.

References

Preface

American Psychiatric Association. (1980). *Diagnostic and statistical manual of mental disorders* (3rd ed.). Arlington, VA: Author.

Kallick, M., Suits, D., Dielman, T., & Hybels, J. (1979). *A survey of American gambling attitudes and behavior*. Ann Arbor: University of Michigan Press.

Kessler, R. C., Hwang, I., LaBrie, R. A., Petukhova, M., Sampson, N., Winters, K., & Shaffer, H. J. (2008). DSM-IV pathological gambling in the National Comorbidity Survey Replication. *Psychological Medicine, 38,* 1351–1360.

Kessler, R. C., & Merikangas, K. R. (2004). The National Comorbidity Survey Replication (NCS-R): Background and aims. *International Journal of Methods in Psychiatric Research, 13,* 60–68.

LaPlante, D. A., Nelson, S. E., LaBrie, R. A., & Shaffer, H. J. (2008). Stability and progression of disordered gambling: Lessons from longitudinal studies. *Canadian Journal of Psychiatry, 53*(1), 52–60.

LaPlante, D. A., & Shaffer, H. J. (2007). Understanding the influence of gambling opportunities: Expanding exposure models to include adaptation. *American Journal of Orthopsychiatry, 77,* 616–623.

National Gambling Impact Study Commission. (1999). *National Gambling Impact Study Commission final report*. Washington, DC: Author.

211

Petry, N. M., Stinson, F. S., & Grant, B. F. (2005). Comorbidity of DSM-IV pathological gambling and other psychiatric disorders: Results from the National Epidemiologic Survey on Alcohol and Related Conditions. *Journal of Clinical Psychiatry, 66,* 564–574.

Pulford, J., Bellringer, M., Abbott, M., Clarke, D., Hodgins, D. C., & Williams, J. (2009). Barriers to help-seeking for a gambling problem: The experiences of gamblers who have sought specialist assistance and the perceptions of those who have not. *Journal of Gambling Studies, 25,* 33–48.

Shaffer, H. J. (2007). Considering the unimaginable: Challenges to accepting self-change or natural recovery from addiction. In H. Klingemann & L. Carter-Sobell (Eds.), *Promoting self-change from addictive behaviors: Practical implications for policy, prevention, and treatment* (2nd ed., pp. ix–xiii). New York: Springer.

Shaffer, H. J., Hall, M. N., & Vander Bilt, J. (1999). Estimating the prevalence of disordered gambling behavior in the United States and Canada: A research synthesis. *American Journal of Public Health, 89,* 1369–1376.

Slutske, W. S. (2006). Natural recovery and treatment-seeking in pathological gambling: Results of two U.S. national surveys. [Brief]. *American Journal of Psychiatry, 163,* 297–302.

Chapter 1: Assessing Your Problems

Kessler, R. C., Hwang, I., LaBrie, R. A., Petukhova, M., Sampson, N., Winters, K. C., & Shaffer, H. J. (2008). DSM-IV pathological gambling in the National Comorbidity Survey Replication. *Psychological Medicine, 38,* 1351–1360.

Petry, N. M., Stinson, F. S., & Grant, B. F. (2005). Comorbidity of DSM-IV pathological gambling and other psychiatric disorders: Results from the National Epidemiologic Survey on Alcohol and Related Conditions. *Journal of Clinical Psychiatry, 66,* 564–574.

Chapter 2: Connecting the Dots

Kessler, R. C., Hwang, I., LaBrie, R. A., Petukhova, M., Sampson, N., Winters, K. C., & Shaffer, H. J. (2008). DSM-IV pathological gambling in the National Comorbidity Survey Replication. *Psychological Medicine, 38,* 1351–1360.

Chapter 4: Getting Your Gambling Under Control

American Psychiatric Association. (2000). *Diagnostic and statistical manual of mental disorders* (4th ed., text rev.). Arlington, VA: Author.

Grant, J. E., Kim, S. W., & Hartman, B. K. (2008) A double-blind, placebo-controlled study of the opiate antagonist naltrexone in the treatment of pathological gambling urges. *Journal of Clinical Psychology*, 69, 783–789.

Ladouceur, R., Jacques, C., Giroux, I., Ferland, F., & Leblond, J. (2000). Analysis of a casino's self-exclusion program. *Journal of Gambling Studies*, 16, 453–460.

Ladouceur, R., Sylvain, C., & Gosselin, P. (2007). Self-exclusion program: A longitudinal evaluation study. *Journal of Gambling Studies*, 23, 85–94.

LaPlante, D. A., Nelson, S. E., LaBrie, R. A., & Shaffer, H. J. (2008). Stability and progression of disordered gambling: Lessons from longitudinal studies. *Canadian Journal of Psychiatry*, 53, 52–60.

Nelson, S. E., Kleschinsky, J. H., LaBrie, R. A., Kaplan, S., & Shaffer, H. J. (2010). One decade of self-exclusion: Missouri casino self-excluders four to ten years after enrollment. *Journal of Gambling Studies*, 26, 129–144.

Chapter 5: Anxiety and Gambling

Kessler, R. C., Hwang, I., LaBrie, R. A., Petukhova, M., Sampson, N., Winters, K. C., & Shaffer, H. J. (2008). DSM-IV pathological gambling in the National Comorbidity Survey Replication. *Psychological Medicine*, 38, 1351–1360.

LaPlante, D. A., Nelson, S. E., LaBrie, R. A., & Shaffer, H. J. (2008). Stability and progression of disordered gambling: Lessons from longitudinal studies. *Canadian Journal of Psychiatry*, 53, 52–60.

Petry, N. M., Stinson, F. S., & Grant, B. F. (2005). Comorbidity of DSM-IV pathological gambling and other psychiatric disorders: Results from the National Epidemiologic Survey on Alcohol and Related Conditions. *Journal of Clinical Psychiatry*, 66, 564–574.

Rickels, K., Zaninelli, R., McCafferty, J., Bellew, J., Iyengar, M., & Sheehan, D. (2003). Paroxetine treatment of generalized anxiety disorder: A double-blind, placebo-controlled study. *American Journal of Psychiatry*, *160*, 749–756.

Chapter 6: Mood Disorders and Gambling

Conway, K. P., Compton, W., Stinson, F. S., & Grant, B. F. (2006). Lifetime comorbidity of DSM-IV mood and anxiety disorders and specific drug use disorders: Results from the National Epidemiologic Survey on Alcohol and Related Conditions. *Journal of Clinical Psychiatry*, *67*, 247–257.

Chapter 7: Impulse Control and Gambling

Kessler, R. C., Hwang, I., LaBrie, R. A., Petukhova, M., Sampson, N. A., Winters, K. C., & Shaffer, H. J. (2008). DSM-IV pathological gambling in the National Comorbidity Survey Replication. *Psychological Medicine*, *38*, 1351–1360.

Koster, E.H.W., Rassin, E., Crombez, G., & Näring, G.W.B. (2003). The paradoxical effects of suppressing anxious thoughts during imminent threat. *Behavior Research and Therapy*, *41*, 1113–1120.

Statistics Canada. (2004). *CANSIM II; series V735319*. E-STAT (Ed.). Ottawa, Ont.: Statistics Canada (producer and distributor).

Wegner, D. M., Schneider, D. J., Carter, S. R., & White, T. L. (1987). Paradoxical effects of thought suppression. *Journal of Personality and Social Psychology*, *53*, 5–13.

Chapter 8: Substance Abuse and Gambling

Compton, W. M., Thomas, Y. F., Stinson, F. S., & Grant, B. F. (2007). Prevalence, correlates, disability, and comorbidity of DSM-IV drug abuse and dependence in the United States: Results from the National Epidemiologic Survey on Alcohol and Related Conditions. *Archives of General Psychiatry*, *64*, 566–576.

Kessler, R. C., Berglund, P., Demler, O., Jin, R., & Walters, E. E. (2005). Lifetime prevalence and age-of-onset distributions of DSM-IV disorders in the National Comorbidity Survey Replication. *Archives of General Psychiatry*, *62*, 593–602.

Marlatt, G. A., & Gordon, J. (Eds.). (1985). *Relapse prevention.* New York: Guilford Press.

Petry, N. M., Stinson, F. S., & Grant, B. F. (2005). Comorbidity of DSM-IV pathological gambling and other psychiatric disorders: Results from the National Epidemiologic Survey on Alcohol and Related Conditions. *Journal of Clinical Psychiatry, 66,* 564–574.

Sobell, L. C., Cunningham, J. A., & Sobell, M. B. (1996). Recovery from alcohol problems with and without treatment: Prevalence in two population surveys. *American Journal of Public Health, 86,* 966–972.

About the Authors

Howard Shaffer, PhD, is an associate professor of psychology at Harvard Medical School and the director of the Division on Addiction at the Cambridge Health Alliance, a Harvard Medical School teaching affiliate. He is also the editor of the American Psychological Association's *Addiction Syndrome Handbook*. He has more than thirty-five years of treatment experience; during his career, he has studied and treated the full range of addiction expressions (for example, gambling, opioids, cocaine, nicotine, shopping, computer, sexual dependence). His clinical and research work has been an influential force in shaping how the field views and treats addiction. In 2010, Shaffer received the American Psychological Association, Division 50, award for Outstanding Contributions to Advancing the Understanding of Addictions.

Ryan Martin, PhD, received his degree from the University of Alabama in 2008. Subsequently, he was awarded the Thomas N. Cummings postdoctoral research fellowship and an appointment through the Harvard Medical School's Department of Psychiatry, the Cambridge Health Alliance's Division on Addiction, and the Massachusetts Council on Compulsive Gambling. Currently, he is an assistant professor in the Department of Health Education and Promotion at East Carolina University. His research interests include mental health and addictive behavior, with a specific focus on gambling behavior.

John Kleschinsky, MPH, received his degree from the University of Massachusetts at Amherst in 2004. Upon completing his master's, he spent three years at the Cambridge Health Alliance's Division on Addiction developing and evaluating public health interventions aimed at preventing and treating a variety of expressions of addiction. Kleschinsky is pursuing a DrPH in social and behavioral sciences at the Boston University School of Public Health. His research interests include addictive behavior, mental health, and the development of dynamic self-help interventions for use on computers and smartphones.

Liz Neporent, MA, is an award-winning health and medical journalist who has written fifteen best-selling health titles. She writes frequently for many national publications and Web sites.

About Harvard Medical School

Since 1782, Harvard Medical School has been an international leader in the effort to improve health care and decrease human suffering from disease. Today more than ten thousand faculty members practice in seventeen affiliated hospitals and research institutions. Harvard Health Publications is the consumer health publishing division of Harvard Medical School and draws on the expertise of faculty members to translate the latest research in order to help individuals improve their health and quality of life.

For more information on Harvard Health Publications, go to http://health.harvard.edu.

Index